# MOSCOW

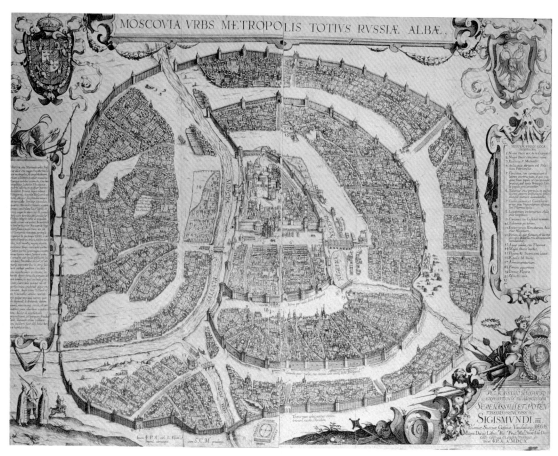

*Moscow. "Sigismund's Plan." 1610*

# MOSCOW

## English Edition

"What is to be compared with this Kremlin, which, surrounded by castellated walls and adorned by the golden domes of cathedrals, sits on a high hill like a royal crown on the head of an awesome monarch?"

"Neither the Kremlin, nor its castellated walls, nor its dark passages, nor its splendid palaces can be described with words... One has to see, to see and to feel everything that they tell one's heart and imagination!"

M.Yu. LERMONTOV *(1814 - 1841)*

ART-RODNIK · *Moscow* · 2 0 0 1

*Text by*
L. K. KORNYUSHOV

*Design and composition by*
L. V. DENISENKO
V. Ya. CHERNIYEVSKY

*Translated from the Russian by*
M. V. NIKOLSKY

*Photos by*
V. N. KORNYUSHIN, I. I. KEITELGISSER, A. I. LAPIN,
V. D. NEKRASOV, I. A. PALMIN,
N. N. RAKHMANOV

ISBN 5 – 88896 – 023 – 3

Printed in NEOGRAFIA, Slovakia

# A GLANCE THROUGH CENTURIES

Moscow is by right considered one of the world capitals that combine in themselves the strength of youth and the wisdom of age. When viewed from the heights of History, eight and a half centuries are a very young age. These 850 years, however, have been so full of events that it would be quite in place to speak about Moscow's special role in the development of human civilisation and, certainly, in the development of Russia. "Those who wish to get to know Russia should visit Moscow," Nikolai Karamzin, the Russian historian, said.

The Russians have always regarded Moscow as the centre from which the power and might of the Russian state developed. Here is a passage from the book *Moscow's Hoary Past*, published in the 19th century: "Moscow gained strength gradually yet steadily, firmly and independently, being Russia's propitiatory sacrifice, as it were, undergoing invasions, ravages, disturbances, fires, and various other popular calamities. Moscow has endured all this owing to its steadfast spirit, owing to its infinite faith, and has become a second Russia, as it were, joining together everything that is dear to the Russian heart." Today these words, uttered over a hundred years ago, still remain no less true than they were then.

Should one wish so, the age of Moscow might be increased by a few centuries. Thus, *A Pantheon of Russian Monarchs* (Volume I) states that Moscow was founded in 880 A. D. That year, it says, Prince Oleg came to the banks of the Moskva River, which was then known as the Smorodina or Smorodinka, and set up a small town at the spot where the Neglinnaya flowed into the Moskva River. Perhaps this is only a legend. Settlements, however, existed on the site of today's Moscow long before that, as recent archaeological excavations have revealed, the most ancient being several thousand years old. The people who inhabited the area were hunters and fishermen living in shelters of straw and leaves and using polished stone and bone tools and weapons.

Traditionally, the age of Moscow is counted from the moment when its formal "birth certificate," its first written mention in the chronicles dating back to 1147, came into existence. In March of that year, Prince Yuri Dolgoruky of Suzdal, gave a lavish feast to his friend and ally Prince Svyatoslav Seversky and a number of other princes in a small settlement named Moscow. At the time, the settlement was owned by Boyar Stepan Kuchko, a highborn and rich man. His house stood near what is now known as Chistiye Prudy and the site of the future Kremlin was grown with an age-old pine forest. Stepan Kuchko owned six settlements: Vorobyovo, Simonovo, Vysotskoye, Kulishki, Kudrino, and Sushchevo. Their names, having stood the test of time, have been preserved to this day in the names of a number of Moscow streets and monasteries.

According to one of the legends, Prince Yuri, passing through Moscow on his way from Kiev to Vladimir in 1156, fell in love with Kuchko's wife. The boyar committed some act injurious to the prince's honour, for which he caused Kuchko to be put to death and confiscated his property. He also married his son Andrei to the boyar's daughter.

This is just one version of the romantic legend of how Moscow was founded. Quite a few others existed as well. The one thing all of them had in common was a love for a beautiful lady and a rivalry between princes for her favours.

Prince Yuri was nicknamed Dolgoruky, "Long-Handed," for his successes in annexing lands in the Northeast of Rus to his possessions. Today his granite likeness sitting astride a battle charger in the centre of Moscow reaches out his mighty hand towards the lands where he went on campaigns in his day.

His countenance is solemn and serious; tradition has it, however, that he was a high-spirited man who was fond of merrymaking. This is what Vasily Tatishchev, the Russian historian, wrote about him: "Yuri, although he had a princess worthy of love and whom indeed he loved, frequently visited the wives of many of his subjects and spent whole nights with them oftener than he did with the princess, playing music and drinking."

**1.** *A view with the Kamenny Bridge from the Zamoskvorechye. Drawing by P. Picart, engraving by J. Blieckland. 1707-1708*

The prince, however, was apparently one of those who have their fun when work is done: he spared no effort increasing his possessions so that his son Andrei inherited, among other lands, the land of Moscow, which was then a minor town in the Suzdal Principality, which, however, had a special strategic importance, for it was here that his subordinate princes mustered their forces when setting out for various parts of the vast Russian lands. Yet neither Prince Andrei himself nor his son Vsevolod lived in Moscow: they only stayed here occasionally. It was only Prince Vladimir, the son of Prince Vsevolod, who established residence in Moscow.

That was when the decades and then centuries of Moscow's unquiet and eventful life full of both troubles and joy began.

In 1238, the city was for the first time burnt down, razed to the ground by Khan Batu. After that the city was many times devastated by foreign foes, yet every time it rose anew from the ashes. The Russian people believed that life itself preserved Moscow, prevented it from sinking to insignificance and prepared it for glory and fame.

Prince Daniil, the son of Alexander Nevsky, the famous Russian prince and military leader who was canonised by the Russian Orthodox Church, was the first to adopt the title of Prince of Moscow. He was a highly intelligent and valiant man admired by the people. He laid the foundation of the Moscow Kremlin, formed a defence force and built quite a few churches and monasteries. He was a schemamonk when he died, having willed to be buried in the graveyard of a cloister that he himself had founded.

Under Prince Daniil's successors Moscow continued to be developed and adorned, and it increased its influence on Russian nationwide affairs. In the reign of his son Grand Duke Ivan Kalita, Metropolitan Pyotr moved house and transferred his cathedra from Vladimir to Moscow. It was also then that the stone Cathedral of the Dormition and Cathedral of the Archangel Michael were laid down and a stone Church of the Saviour was built in place of a wooden one.

Moscow's superiority over the other Russian cities was finally established during the reign of Grand Duke Dimitry, later on nicknamed Donskoi.

Moscow had grown so much that now it was divided into five parts: the Kremlin (the citadel), the Kitaigorod (the inner city), the Posad (the merchants' and artisans' quarter, subsequently known as the White City), the Zarechye (the district lying beyond the Moskva River), and the Zagorodye (subsequently known as the Earthworks City).

At the time, not only the first stone churches were built, but also quite a few other things were for the first time made in Moscow. A Russian craftsman by the name of Boriska cast the first three bells. It was also then that Moscow's first cloisters—the Monastery of the Archangel Michael's Miracle at Chonae, the Monastery of Our Saviour built by St. Andronik, the Simonov Monastery, and the Convent of the Ascension—were founded. In the reign of Grand Duke Vasily, the son of Dimitry Donskoi, the first cannon were made and the first tower clock was installed in the grand duke's courtyard.

2

And all the time Moscow had to repulse the raids of belligerent invaders from the wild steppes—Tamerlane, Yedigei, and other major and minor khans. It was bled white, it paid enormous tributes, its citizens were driven into slavery. And yet it held out!

In those days Moscow acquired its own holy guardian and protectress. This is how it happened. In 1395, Tamerlane leading an immense horde approached Moscow. Grand Duke Vasily and his men were ready to give battle to the enemy, but they would have had to fight against heavy odds. The Muscovites then decided to pray to God for help and brought an icon of the Mother of God from Vladimir to Moscow, receiving it with great honours. Nearly all the citizens of Moscow gathered on the Kuchkovo Field, the place where their city had been founded centuries ago. There they prayed before the icon for a long time and then carried it to the Kremlin Cathedral of the Dormition. Having learnt about this, Tamerlane stopped his troops and eventually ordered them to retreat from Moscow without a fight. After that, as old books have it, "as a token of gratitude to the All-Mighty and to keep eternally alive the memory of the occasion, the Muscovites instituted a Feast of the Meeting of the Mother of God, to be celebrated on August 26 (Old Style.—Ed.)." A monastery was built on the Kuchkovo Field.

Ever since, the Vladimir Icon of the Mother of God has been regarded as the protectress of Moscow.

Moscow withstood raids made on it by nomads, fought fires and epidemics, and passed through periods of vehement strife and violent clashes in the struggle for the throne and power. Naturally, all these events determined the tenor of life in the rapidly growing city for years and sometimes for decades. In the course of time, however, all of them became things of the past.

There were also events that had a centuries-long influence on the life of the city, and they became major historical landmarks in the annals of Moscow. In 1433, Grand Duke Yuri permitted Bishop Serafimy to build a stone house, the first stone dwelling house to be built in Moscow, and this was the beginning of the stone city. During the reign of Grand Duke Ivan III, Moscow forever refused to pay a tribute to the Golden Horde. Ivan III

*2. Railway station.*
*A view*
*of the Nikolayevsky*
*Railway Station and*
*Kalanchyovskaya Square.*
*Lithograph*
*by L.-J. Jacottet*
*and Aubrun from*
*an original*
*by A. J. Charlemagne.*
*1850s*

**3.** *Part of the Tainitsky Gardens in the Kremlin with the Church of Sts. Constantine and Helen, viewed in the direction of the Moskvoretsky Bridge. Colour lithograph. Late 19th-early 20th centuries*

destroyed the khan's pai-tzu plaque and slew his envoys, having set free one of them, whom he ordered to return to the Horde with the following message for the khan: "The hen that laid golden eggs for the Tatars has died." Thus in 1480 Ivan ended the formal subservience of the Muscovite rulers to the Tatars.

During his reign, Novgorod and Tver were annexed to Muscovy and the city of Kazan was conquered for the first time.

After he had married Zoë (Sophia) Palaeologus, niece of the last emperor of Byzantium, the grand duke adopted the state emblem of the Byzantine Empire, a black double-headed eagle, as the emblem of the Moscow Grand Duchy. It was also during his reign that police was for the first time instituted in Moscow. By a special ukase September 1 instead of March 1 was adopted as the first day of the year. A legal code known as Sudebnik (Code of Laws) was published.

Ivan III was a reformer and his reign was marked by quite a few improvements, even though a number of calamities such as fires and a severe earthquake, the only one in the entire history of Moscow, befell the city during that period, casting a shadow on those otherwise trouble-free years.

In the early 16th century, Moscow was already well-known all over the world. At the time, it was a big city with a character all its own, a city with a population of more than 100,000. Grand Duke Vasily III of Moscow began to call himself "ruler of all Russia."

Not a single one of the eight and a half centuries of Moscow's history passed without hardships and trials befalling the city, yet its people always showed firmness of spirit, indus-

**4.** *Parade in the Kremlin in 1839. Artist G. Chernetsov. 1841*

try and an ability to bear up against misfortune—in a word, what is known as the Muscovite character.

In 1571, the Crimean Khan Davlet Girei laid siege to Moscow and the Tatars set fire to the city. Within the space of three hours, the city was burnt to the ground and more than 120,000 troops and civilians perished in the fire. The Muscovites, however, built their city anew. Moscow was burnt down dozens of times, yet palaces and mansions were built in it even in periods of foreign invasions and popular unrest. Even False Dimitry, the pretender to the Russian throne, managed to build a palace decorated with enormous lions. As a matter of fact, these lions, which amazed and shocked the Muscovites, are believed to have contributed to the sharp decline in his popularity with the masses.

Moscow always guarded Russia's interests and Russia, when this was needed, came to Moscow's rescue. Early in the 17th century, popular volunteer troops led by Kozma Minin, a citizen of Nizhni Novgorod, and Prince Dmitry Pozharsky, blessed by Patriarch Hermogen, advanced on Moscow in order to scour foreign invaders from the capital.

Since then, Moscow has only once been seized by foreign troops: this was in 1812 when Napoleon's Grande Armée attempted to conquer Russia.

Peter the Great, the Russian emperor famous for his sweeping reforms, transferred the capital of the Russian state from Moscow to St. Petersburg, yet he preserved its title of a first-cathedra and capital city. In the days of Peter the Great, Moscow was adorned with a number of new, beautiful buildings such as the Sukhareva Tower and the Poteshny Palace. It was precisely in the Petrine times that Moscow shook off patriarchal drowsiness charac-

11

teristic of the Old Russian life style and began to look more like a European city.

Each of the emperors and empresses who reigned after Peter the Great regarded it as their duty to leave a good memory of themselves in Moscow by building new cathedrals, palaces and administrative buildings.

If you take a look at Moscow from the two tallest structures in its centre, the 81-metre-high Ivan the Great Bell Tower and the Cathedral of Christ the Saviour, you will see that the vast city is arranged in several rings with a series of thoroughfares radiating out from its centre.

The Kremlin is the natural "nucleus" from which Moscow started to grow. First, the merchants' settlement lying next to the Kremlin—the citadel—was surrounded with a towered wall. This area was given the name "Kitai-gorod" (from the Old Slavonic kita, which meant a bundle of stakes, for these bundles formed the basis of the earthworks which surrounded the original area). The second fortification ring, built round the Kremlin and Kitaigorod, enclosed a whole new part of Moscow, which became known as the Bely Gorod (White City). Later on, an earthen rampart was erected round a much larger area, the Zemlyanoi Gorod (Earthworks City). Finally, in 1742 the Kamer-Kollezhsky Rampart was built. Thus, there were four rings round the Kremlin, which played both a defensive and an economic role.

**5.** *A view of the mansion of the military governor-general. Lithograph by J.-B. Arnout. Daziaro Publishing House. 1850s*

Kitaigorod was originally known as Posad (Trading Quarter), for it was tradespeople who had been ousted from the Kremlin by the local nobility. Its boundaries were clearly outlined: the Neglinnaya River on its northern side, the Moskva River on its southern side, and the Kremlin on its west. Its eastern side was defended with earthen and wooden fortifications. It had for a long time been Moscow's trading centre. In 1535-1538, this area was surrounded with a six-metre high and about six-metre thick stone wall stretching for of 2,600 metres. Running round the wall along its top was a walkway and above the wall there were 14 towers, six of which had gateways in them. By the beginning of the 20th century, Kitaigorod had become the area where all Moscow's major banking and commercial business was transacted. "No other district in Moscow is as busy, rich and populous as Kitaigorod is," said a guidebook to Moscow dating from 1903. People fond of foreign words dubbed this district of Moscow 91 hectares in area "Moscow's City." It was also probably the most colourful district in Moscow where simple and small shops stood side by side with great shopping arcades, rich banks, offices of prospering trade and industry companies, the mansion of the Romanov Boyars, the old Synodal Printing House, and a number of churches and monasteries. Today this district is one of the old parts of Moscow protected by the state.

The Kitaigorod wall was pulled down in 1936, in the period of total reconstruction of the city.

The Bely Gorod—the White City—grew round the Kremlin and Kitaigorod out of suburban settlements and boyars' landed estates interspersed with churches and cloisters such as the St. Aleksy Convent, the Convent of Great Martyr St. Nicetas and the Convent of St. John the Baptist that had appeared amidst one-time dense forests. This area reached its heyday in the 15th century.

12

The White City and its inhabitants were the first to fall victim to nomads' raids on Moscow. And so, after the invasion carried out by the Crimean Khan Davlet Girei in 1571, when the White City was burnt to the ground and its residents were slaughtered or driven away to be sold for slaves, a mighty stone wall with 28 towers and nine gates was built round it. The White City included artisans' settlements—Lubyanka (Bast-Makers'), Kuznechnaya (Blacksmiths'), Kolokolnaya (Bell-Casters'), and a number of others. Besides, rich merchants lived here and in the mid-18th century noblemen, including such well-known families as the Sheremetevs, the Yusupovs, the Golitsyns, and others, began to establish residence in this area.

Little by little, however, the walls of the White City fell into decay, nomads' raids became a thing of the past, and the Empress Elizabeth Petrovna caused the walls and towers to be pulled down. Later on, the Empress Catherine the Great ordered to lay boulevards in place of the pulled-down walls. Thus the Boulevards Ring, a favourite spot among Muscovites, came into being.

There is a supposition that the outline of the present-day Garden Ring with the curve of the Moskva River inside it looks very much like the representation of a mute swan which is to be seen on copper ornaments that the ancient pagan Slavs, very distant ancestors of today's Russians, used to wear. They regarded the mute swan as a symbol of the Sun. Not long ago, archaeologists carrying on excavations in Moscow uncovered a copper bracelet showing a woman with her arms raised, with solar disks ornamented with swan heads on her sides. The swans' curved necks were turned upwards. No one has been able to explain what the similarity between the contours of Moscow's Garden Ring and the representation of an ancient Slav deity can mean. There is, however, still another striking coincidence: the number of solar rays spreading out from the representation of the Sun exactly corresponds to the number of gates built in the walls of the White City. What is it: a new legend, an accidental coincidence or a discovery?

6. *The Imperial Bolshoi Theatre in Moscow. Lithograph by A. Cadolle. Ca. 1825*

The Earthworks City lay between the present-day Boulevards Ring and Garden Ring. Living within its wall, which formed Moscow's first line of defence, were Ivan the Terrible's oprichniki (officers of the governmental punitive force instituted by the tsar), and also artisans and servicemen, who resided in settlements that were known by their occupation—Konyushennaya (Harnessers'), Ikonnaya (Icon-Painters'), Plotnichya (Carpenters'), Povarskaya (Cooks'), and so on. This part of the city was built over in a chaotic manner: people built whatever and wherever they wanted. Quite a few houses were built of logs, prepared in advance, within the space of two days. Such houses were dubbed skorodom, literally meaning a "fast house." To protect the area, a 15 kilometres long and nearly five metres high wooden wall with numerous wooden towers was built round it late in the 16th century. The entire fortification burnt down in 1611. In 1638, an earthen rampart was erected to protect the area, which since then began to be called the Zemlyanoi Gorod, the Earthworks City. Two decades later, a wooden wall with towers was once again built here. A deep moat and a high rampart topped with a wall built of logs one metre thick formed a formidable defence line. This ring encompassed the city of Moscow, now covering an area of 1,887 hectares.

In the course of time, noblemen, retired civil servants and merchants began to take up residence in the Earthworks City. Even dignitaries built spacious manors and palaces here, buying plots of land for a song. After the great fire during the Patriotic War of 1812 against Napoleon, Moscow began to be built anew. In the process, the Earthen Rampart was pulled down and a 20 to 25 metres wide circular street round Moscow was laid in its place. Thus the present-day Garden Ring was formed.

Moscow's growth did not stop with the Earthworks City: it soon overstepped its boundaries and continued to expand, turning the nearby forests and fields into town estates and suburban settlements.

7

New suburbs such as Nemetskaya Sloboda (German Suburb) and Meshchanskaya Sloboda (Petty Bourgeois Suburb), and the settlements of the Preobrazhensky, Semyonovsky, Lefortov and other regiments emerged outside the Earthworks City. Tollgates were put up on major roads leading to the city, and Moscow's customs boundary, previously passing along the Earthen Rampart, was moved to their line. Rows of wooden posts were erected in the intervals between the tollgates. The purposes of this measure were purely commercial; one of them was an attempt to stop the smuggling of vodka, which could only be sold by establishments having a licence from the state. This, however, did not help, for the local inhabitants fell into the habit of stealing the posts to use them as fuel for their stoves. And so Moscow was surrounded with a moat and an earthen rampart along that line, which was now patrolled by mounted guards. The decision on this had been adopted by the Kammer-Kollegium, a very influential government agency established by Peter the Great in his day. It was after this agency that the new rampart was called Kamer-Kollezhsky. Encompassing the whole of Moscow, it was 35

*7. A view of the Cathedral of Christ the Saviour. Early 20th century*

versts long (the verst, a unit of length used in Russia at the time, was equal to 1.067 kilometres or 0.6629 mile). Crossing it were artery roads leading to Tver, Serpukhov and other cities. In all, there were 18 such roads with tollgates.

The area inside the Kamer-Kollezhsky Rampart came to 7,089 hectares, and it was Now not only the customs, but also the police boundary of Moscow, separating the city from the Moscow Gubernia.

In view of Moscow's continued growth it was decided to dismantle the Kamer-Kollezhsky Rampart, and this work lasted for nearly the entire second half of the 19th century. Today the word val, "rampart," is to be found in the names of quite a few Moscow streets such as Preobrazhensky Val, Izmailovsky Val, etc.

Nowadays Moscow's four rings are not so clearly outlined on the city map as they were in the 19th century. Yet it is these rings that played a major part first in the city's defence and then in its development. In addition to them there was a locality on the right-hand bank of the Moskva River opposite the Kremlin—the Zamoskvorechye, the name meaning "area beyond the Moskva River." In the 18th century, merchants ousted from the Kremlin began to settle here next to artisans' and servicemen's districts.

It should also be added that in the distant outskirts the city, built over the centuries in a simple yet solid manner, was protected by several monasteries doubling as fortified outposts: the Monastery of Our Saviour built by St. Andronik, the easternmost of them, the Novospassky (New Monastery of the Saviour) and the Simonov Monasteries on the left-

14

hand bank of the Moskva River, the St. Daniel Monastery on its right-hand bank, and the Novodevichy Convent on Moscow's western side.

In the late 18th-early 19th centuries, Moscow, which was then a very big city by the yard-stick of the day, was divided into 20 sections and 88 districts. It had 131 streets, 471 lanes, 9 cathedrals, 24 monasteries and convents, 325 churches, 8,426 stone and wooden houses, more than 1,100 shops, 233 plants, 147 factories, and a population of nearly 217,000.

At the turn of the 20th century Moscow was in its prime. Its industry, finances and trade were on the rise. It enjoyed a high international prestige and maintained extensive ties with dozens of countries of the world.

In the early 20th century, Moscow surpassed many of the world capitals both in area and in the size of population. The length of its boundary came to 80.5 versts and its popu-lation exceeded 2,000,000. The city was no less civilised than any other major city in Europe. Here is what one of the contemporaries wrote about Moscow at the time: "Small courtyards of a provincial type like the one immortalised by Polenov are becoming ever fewer, whereas courtyards with gardens are growing in number. Orchards are being cut clear and wooden cottages are giving place either to grand mansions or to multistorey blocks of flats. And the old-time types depicted by Ostrovsky have nearly become extinct: the peaked cap and the top hat have been replaced with the bowler and the frock coat with the dinner jacket and the cutaway; we now see American-made elastic-sides instead of bot-tle-shaped boots and clean-shaven faces or beards trimmed in the European fashion instead of spade beards; even famous merchants' equipages presided over by a stomachy coachman and drawn by spirited steeds are being ousted by motorcars…"

Moscow was looking ahead with confidence. In the 20th century, however, three rev-olutions and four devastating wars (the Russo-Japanese War of 1904-1905, the First World War, the Civil War of 1918-1920, and the Great Patriotic War of 1941-1945) befell Russia and Moscow. Great revolutionary and social cataclysms tossed the country and its capital like a ship in a storm. In the 20th century Moscow got its full share of everything—great fame, bitter losses and dramatic historical turns. The violent tempest of the revolution of 1917 is without parallel in world history, just as the monstrous atrocities of the nazi aggres-sion are beyond compare. At the same time, however, examples of similarly rapid growth of a great city and of a similarly tremendous scope of its reconstruction and renovation, sometimes hasty yet always directed towards the future, are hardly a common occurrence.

Moscow is often described as beautiful. This is precisely what people call it: Moscow the Beautiful. Moscow is one of the rare cases of a city preserving its beauty in perpetuity, whatever happens. Enjoying the love of the whole nation, it emerged renewed out of every fresh bitter trial, as if sprinkled with holy water.

To those who get to know Moscow closely and with respect, it is quite evident that today Moscow with its history, its architectural masterpieces and its innumerable art trea-sures has found itself at a boundary between two different eras, in a whirlpool of global currents determining world development.

Moscow is approaching the end of the 20th century as a city radically different from what it was at the turn of the century. You may change the names of streets and squares to what they once were and restore a couple of dozen buildings that were foolishly demol-ished, but you cannot turn back the clock.

What does Moscow, an all-time favourite of the Russian people, look like today?

This is what this album will tell you about.

THE PRESENT-DAY KREMLIN is a gem of Russian architecture which has been taking shape for centuries, an ensemble of wonderful palaces and cathedrals, a treasure house in which collections of values absolutely beyond compare are kept. "The Kremlin is a place of great historical remembrances," is what Nikolai Karamzin, the Russian historian, said about it. When looking at the magnificent panorama of the Kremlin, it is hard to believe that this area was covered with dense forests at one time.

In the hoary past, the central part of Old Russian cities surrounded with walls and towers was called detinets. It was only in the 14th century that the word kremlin, meaning "citadel," came into use and has since then been part of the Russian language. A kremlin was usually situated on an eminence by a river.

The Vyatichi, one of the Slavic tribes that were the ancestors of the Russians, founded the

Moscow Kremlin on the Borovitsky Hill on the left-hand bank of the Moskva River.

Originally, a small settlement of merchants and artisans with a circular fortification round it was built on top of this hill amidst a mighty bor, pine forest—hence the name of the hill. At the same time or a little bit later, a second centre of the settlement, also fortified, sprang up on the southwestern shoulder of the hill. The fortifications included a moat, a rampart and a stockade. Some time round the mid-11th century, the two centres merged into a single fort whose walls ran along the Neglinnaya River to the spot where the Troitskiye Gates are situated today, then skirted the area of today's Cathedral Square and extended south and west, closing the line of defences. The walls, which were constructed out of long oaken logs on top of an earthen rampart, enclosed an area not more than one-tenth of the present-day Kremlin grounds. Inside the

**8.** *The architectural ensemble of the Moscow Kremlin*

8

fort were the dwelling houses of the prince, his kinfolk and members of his fighting force and, probably, a wooden church. Situated outside the walls was the posad—the merchants' and artisans' quarter.

Some scholars believe that as early as the end of the 13th century there was a stone church in honour of St. Demetrios inside the fortress on the Borovitsky Hill. Today the Cathedral of the Dormition stands on its site.

9. *A view of the Kremlin cathedrals*

10. *Vodovzvodnaya Tower*

According to the chronicles, it was in 1331 that the fortress began to be known as the Kremlin. The wooden Kremlin was burnt to the ground more than once during raids of nomadic tribes, yet each time it was built anew. In the reign of Grand Duke Ivan Kalita (first half of the 14th century), Moscow became prominent as the centre of unification of the Russian lands, which had an effect on the Kremlin. Ivan Kalita transferred the see of the Russian metropolitans to Moscow

and the first stone churches—the Cathedral of the Dormition, the Church of the Saviour-on-the-Pine-Forest and the Church of St. John Climacus—were built on the Kremlin grounds. In the days of Ivan Kalita, over a period of two years, 1339 and 1340, new oaken walls one metre thick were put up round the Kremlin.

The present-day Kremlin has the shape of an irregular triangle 27.5 hectares in area, somewhat reminiscent of a heart. It took many centuries to build it. In 1367, Grand Duke Dimitry Donskoi ordered that the oaken walls should be replaced with walls made of beautiful yet not very durable white stone. It was then that the Kremlin surrounded the posad (merchants' and artisans' quarter) and nearly the entire area it covers today. Six gate towers rose above the walls. Seen against the background of blue sky and green forests surrounding the Kremlin, its white-stone cathedrals and mansions presented a wondrously beautiful sight. It was then that such expressions as "white-stone Moscow" and "the great and wonderful city of Moscow" came into use.

Dimitry Donskoi's Kremlin stood for a century. The white-stone Kremlin walls, however, were gradually crumbling, and so in 1485 the construction of new, stronger walls was launched. They were built of big and heavy red brick (each brick weighing 8.5 kilograms). The height of the walls depended on the relief of the area, ranging from 19 to 5 metres. The top of the walls was protected with 2 to 2.5 metres high and 70 to 85 centimetres thick bifurcated merlons. There were a total of 1,045 such merlons having the elegant form of a swallow's tail. The merlons are provided with loopholes and the walls have embrasures for heavy cannon to fire through. A walkway 2 to 4 metres wide was made along the top of the walls, which in olden times was covered with ridged wooden roofing. The walls, spanning a total of 2,235 metres, ran from one tower to another, each of them having its own purpose.

Making the designs and supervising the construction work, executed by skillful Russian masons, carpenters and ironmasters, were Italian engineers and architects Marco Fryazin (Marco Ruffo), Pietro Antonio Solari and Antonio and Aleviz (Aloisio) Fryazin.

While the walls and towers of the Kremlin have stood for several centuries, with only some repairs or restoration work done on them from time to time, there have been constant changes among the buildings standing on its grounds: they were built and then pulled down to be replaced with other, new ones.

**11.** *The Kutafya and Troitskaya (Trinity) Towers*

**12.** *The Borovitskaya Tower*

All the twenty KREMLIN TOWERS are very different from one another. The corner towers are round and those along the walls are rectangular. Eighteen towers are built into the fortress walls. One turret, called the Tsarskaya (Tsar's) Tower (situated opposite the Cathedral of St. Vasily the Blessed), is placed on the wall. Still another one, the Kutafya Tower, stands separately in front of the Troitskaya Tower and is linked with it by a bridge. The heavy, squat Kutafya Tower was thus named either because in days of old the word kutafya used to mean "dumpy woman" or its name was derived from the word kut, meaning "nook."

The Troitskaya (Trinity) Tower, built in 1495, changed its name several times. Known originally as Bogoyavlenskaya (Epiphany), it was later on renamed the Rizpolozhenskaya (Deposition of the Robe), Znamenskaya (after the Icon of the Mother of God "The Sign"), and Karetnaya (Coach) Tower. The tower is 69.3 metres high.

20

The Borovitskaya (Predtechenskaya) Gate Tower was built to the design of Pietro Anronio Solari in 1490. In front of its gate there used to be a bridge over the Neglinnaya River. The name of the tower comes from the word bor, "pine forest," which once covered the whole Kremlin (or Borovitsky) Hill and the area round it. The tower has three progressively smaller square tiers built on its massive rectangular lower part, distinguishing it from the other Kremlin towers.

In 1488, another round tower, the Sviblova Tower, named after Boyar Sviblov, was built at the spot where the Neglinnaya River used to flow into the Moskva River. In 1633, a water elevating machine that supplied the Kremlin with water was installed in this tower; hence its second, present name, the Vodovzvodnaya Tower (Water Tower).

The building of the Arsenal was erected in

13

**13.** *The building of the Arsenal. The Kremlin*

**14.** *A view of the Kremlin towers*

**15.** *Cathedral Square in the Kremlin* ▷

1702-1736 by architects M. Choglokov, M. Remizov, and a number of others. A year later, however, the Arsenal was severely damaged during a great fire in the Kremlin. In 1786-1796, it was restored by engineer L. I. Gerard under the supervision of the architect Matvei Kazakov. In 1812, the building was once again damaged—this time, by a blowup during the retreat of Napoleon's troops from Moscow. It was later on restored by architects I. L. Mironovsky, A. N. Bakarev, and others. It was then that the present appearance of the Arsenal, a structure built in the Classicist style, austere-looking yet expressive in its way, took its final shape.

Along the building of the Arsenal, 875 trophy cannons captured by the Russian troops during the retreat of Napoleon's Grande Armée in 1812 were placed in the mid-19th century. In 1960, a number of Russian cannons from the Armoury's collections of weapons were added to them.

The main and the oldest square in the Kremlin is CATHEDRAL SQUARE that has witnessed all the most important events in the history of the Russian state. It was here that the august personages greeted foreign ambassadors and the ceremonial processions from the Cathedral of the Dormition were held when the tsars were crowned and on other major occasions. Surrounding it are the Ivan the Great Bell Tower, the Palace of Facets, the Cathedrals of the Dormition, the Annunciation and the Archangel Michael, and a number of other monuments of Russian architecture.

17

The focal point of the Kremlin architectural ensemble is THE IVAN THE GREAT BELL TOWER. Originally the bell tower, built by the architect Bon Fryazin in 1505-1508, consisted of the two lower tiers and, partially, the third tier of the presently existing tower and was 60 metres high. In olden times, it served as the Kremlin's watchtower and signal tower. It was given its name, "Ivan," after St. John Climacus to whom the church inside the first tier of the bell tower is dedicated, and was dubbed "the Great" on account of its unusually great height. In 1532-1543, the architect Petrok Maly built a campanile close to the northern façade of the bell tower. In 1600, Tsar Boris Godunov ordered to add another tier on top of the bell tower, which, after it had been completed, reached a height of 81 metres and in 1624 the Filaret Annex was added to the Ivan the Great complex. Today there are a total of 21 bells dating from the 16th to 19th centuries in the bell tower and campanile, the biggest of them weighing 70 tons.

THE TEREM PALACE (the word terem means "upper chambers of a palace") was built on the orders of Tsar Mikhail Fyodorovich Romanov by Russian master builders Bazhen Ogurtsov, Larion Ushakov, and others in 1635-1636.

**16.** *The Ivan the Great Bell Tower and the campanile*

**17.** *The Terem Palace*

**18.** *Tsar Cannon. 1586*

18

**19.** *The cupolas of the royal domestic churches in the Terem Palace. 17th century*

**20.** *Tsar Bell. 1733-1735*

**21.** *The Cathedral of the Annunciation*

The ensemble of the Terem Palace includes several churches, which used to serve as private chapels of the royal family. In 1682, they were covered with a single roof and topped with eleven cupolas on slender drums decorated with tiles (architect Osip Startsev, tiles by master Ippolit). The cupolas are above the Verkhospassky Cathedral (Upper Cathedral of the Saviour) dedicated to the Image of the Saviour "Not Made with Hands" (1635-1636), the Church of the Resurrection of Christ (1680-1681),

and the Church of the Crucifixion (1681).

The interiors of the Terem churches a number of superb 17th-century art masterpieces have been preserved. They include the carved gilt wooden iconostasis by Russian artists (Verkhospassky Cathedral) and icons by Fyodor Zubov, Simon Ushakov and other leading masters of the royal workshops. Quite unique is the iconostasis in the Church of the Crucifixion with icons where the background and the garments are made of

West European and Oriental silk and brocade fabrics using the appliqué technique (artist Vasily Poznansky).

THE CATHEDRAL OF THE ANNUNCIATION (1484-1489), the domestic church of the Moscow grand dukes and the Russian tsars, was built of bricks by master builders from Pskov on the white-stone crypt of an older church, dating from 1397, which had been pulled down.

The cathedral was originally three-domed. In the second half of the 16th century, the cathedral was rebuilt: the open galleries were closed over with vaults upon which four small single-domed side chapels were erected, and another two domes were added on its western side.

Inside the Cathedral of the Annunciation a 15th-century iconostasis, one of the oldest in Russia, has survived with priceless icons believed to be works by such famous Russian icon-painters as Andrei Rublev, Theophanes the Greek and starets (the word starets means "elder" or "spiritual father") Prokhor of Gorodets.

20

21

**22.** *The Cathedral of the Archangel Michael. The interior*

**23.** *The Cathedral of the Dormition. The interior*

**24.** *The Divine Liturgy is being celebrated on the day of the Feast of the Nativity of Christ in the Cathedral of the Dormition*

24

THE CATHEDRAL OF THE ARCHANGEL MICHAEL (1505-1508, architect Aleviz Novy or Aloisio the New) served as the family burial place for the Moscow grand dukes and the Russian tsars.

In 1679-1681, a new four-tiered gilt iconostasis was built in the cathedral. Set in it are old icons dating from the 14th to 18th centuries.

THE CATHEDRAL OF THE DORMITION (1475-1479, architect Aristotle Fioravanti) has for centuries been regarded as the main church in Moscow. Russian metropolitans and patriarchs lie buried here.

In 1482, the cathedral was decorated with the participation of Dionisy, the famous iconpainter. The interior of the cathedral is decorated with wall paintings dating from 1642-1643 and a five-tiered iconostasis covered with embossed gilt silver. The unique masterpieces that are to be seen in the cathedral include the icon St. George the Victorious, an outstanding monument of 12th-century Russian art, the Icon of the Saviour "The Fiery Eye" (mid-14th century), and a number of others.

THE GRAND KREMLIN PALACE is a rare example of Russian architecture of the second half of the 19th century. This majestic building was built on the crest of the Borovitsky Hill in its southwestern part, which once was the site of the grand dukes' and, later on, of the tsars' residence.

The first mention of palatial structures in the Kremlin dates back to the 14th century and is linked to the name of Grand Duke Ivan Kalita. The inexorable course of time and numerous fires and did not spare the ancient Kremlin structures, and by the end of the 18th century many of the surviving ones became dilapidated. The construction of a new palace that would meet the requirements of the imperial family was launched in 1838 and continued for eleven years.

The main façade of the palace faces the Moskva River. A group of architects headed by the well-known St. Petersburg architect Konstantin Ton (1794-1881) were commissioned to design and build the palace. A number of prominent Moscow architects such as F. F. Richter, N. I. Chichagov, P. A. Gerasimov, and others also took part in its construction. They succeeded in combining such distinct Kremlin structures dating from different periods (14th-17th centuries) as the Palace of Facets, the Tsarina's Golden Chamber, the Terem Palace and the palace churches, as well as the newly-built 19th century Grand Kremlin Palace into a single whole.

The architects decorated the palace building with carved white-stone pediments and platbands over the window openings with double arches connected by a tie piece "hanging" in the middle, after the fashion of 17th-century terem palaces. The palace is covered with a hipped roof and has a rectangular attic topped with a dome. Its main façade is 125 metres long and 44 metres high. The palace contains nearly 700 separate rooms with a total floor area of about 20,000 square metres. The building appears to be three stories high, but in fact there are only two, the upper having its windows in two tiers.

Its splendid 19th-century interiors, which have almost completely been preserved to this day, are designed in a variety of styles ranging from the Baroque to classicism. Characteristic of the artistic treatment its rooms and halls is regal splendour and exceptional perfection of execution.

25

**25.** *The Grand Kremlin Palace*

Alongside architects, a number of noted painters and sculptors such as Fyodor Solntsev, Ivan Vitali, Pyotr Klodt, and Alexander Loganovsky were commissioned to decorate the palace's interiors. Furniture and elements of interior decoration were made to their sketches at a number of well-known Russian plants, factories and workshops.

The ceremonial reception halls—the Georgievsky (St. George), Vladimirsky (St. Vladimir), Andreyevsky (St. Andrew), Alexandrovsky (St. Alexander) and Yekaterininsky (St. Catherine) Halls—occupy the entire first floor of the Grand Kremlin Palace. Their names correspond to orders that used to exist in Russia before the revolution. Included in the stucco ornamentation of the halls are representations of the insignia of the respective orders and the upholstery features the colours of their ribbons.

Next to the Georgievsky Hall, the biggest of

**26.** *The grand staircase in the Grand Kremlin Palace*

26

the palace's ceremonial halls (it is 61 metres long, 20.5 metres wide and 17.5 metres high), is the Vladimirsky Hall dedicated to the Order of St. Vladimir instituted by Catherine the Great in 1782. It was built on the site of the 17th-century open-air Boyar Square of the Terem Palace. Today it links the 15th-17th century palatial buildings with the newer ones, dating from the 19th century. Shaped like a square with cut-off corners in plan, this hall consists of large

ed for holding party congresses and sessions of the Supreme Soviet. At present, they are being restored.

The first floor of the Grand Kremlin Palace on its western side is occupied by an enfilade of the so-called Ceremonial Quarters rooms—the Yekaterininsky Hall, the State Drawing-room, the Royal Bedchamber, and the Walnut Dressing Room.

The next one after the light silver-gray Yeka-

27

**27.** *The State Bedchamber.*

*Northern part*

**28.** *The Vladimirsky*

*(St. Vladimir) Hall*

wide arches in the lower part on top of which are smaller arches with galleries behind them. The walls and pilasters of the hall are faced with pink artificial marble. It is topped with a dome-like vault ornamented with a gilt pattern and representations of the insignia of the Order of St. Vladimir. The floor in the hall is decorated with parquet made of rare woods to sketches by the painter Fyodor Solntsev.

In 1934, the Andreyevsky and Alexandrovsky Halls were combined into one huge hall intend-

terininsky Hall, which used to serve as the throne room of the Russian empresses, is the State Drawing-room. The vaulted ceiling of this semicircular hall was ornamented with a flowered pattern by painter D. Artari. The walls and furniture in it are upholstered in golden-green brocade. The tables and palisander mirror doors of the Drawing-room feature the buhl style (after André-Charles Boulle, or Buhl, the famous royal cabinetmaker at Versailles in the reign of Louis XIV). The furniture is inlaid with brass,

pewter, mother-of-pearl, tortoiseshell, and various woods. The niches in this room are faced with white artificial marble. They contain porcelain standard lamps painted with exquisite patterns in a "Chinese" style.

In the interior decoration of the Royal Bedchamber wide use is made of natural and artificial marble of a variety of colours—white, pinkish-grey, and green. The main adornments of this room are monolithic columns of greenish-

creating an atmosphere of comfort and intimacy. Each room is ornamented with exquisite gilded stucco moulding on the vaulted ceilings and cornices and on the capitals of the pilasters and columns, which makes them look particularly festive. Each of the seven rooms—the Dining-room, the Drawing-room, the Empress's Study, the Boudoir, the Bedroom, the Emperor's Study, the Reception Room—and four small rooms serving as passageways are unique exam-

**29.** *The Private Chambers.*

*Bedroom*

**30.** *The State Drawing-Room.*

*Eastern part*

29

grey marble and a mantel faced with jasper of bluish-green hues.

On the ground floor of the palace are the Private Chambers—the imperial family's private apartments—forming a straight enfilade with windows looking south. In decorating the interiors of the rooms, decorative pieces of various styles such as classicism, the Baroque and rococo are used. Skilfully arranged period furniture, richly ornamented with inlaid work, harmonises well with the space of the rooms,

ples of 19th-century interior decoration. Each of them has a distinctive appearance all its own thanks to the use different materials in decorating their interiors and the skilful, careful choice of articles of porcelain, crystal and bronze and fabrics of rare beauty and exceptional quality.

The enfilade of the Private Chambers opens with the Dining-room, the biggest and lightest of them. Each one of the rooms that follow, beginning with the Drawing-room, is divided

into two distinct parts differing in size and purpose. The front part with windows and mantels, situated on the axis of the enfilade, has a grander décor. The other part, the one at the back, was intended for home activities and rest.

The Bedroom has a more austere décor; its walls and modest furniture are covered with blue moire. Predominating in its colour scheme are three colours—blue, white and gold. The ceiling is exquisitely painted with bouquets and intricate floral patterns. The room has a beautiful mantel of white marble with a traditional mantel clock and candelabra on the shelf.

Today the Grand Kremlin Palace remains one of the major centres of state life in Russia. Summit meetings, and diplomatic receptions, presentations of government awards and other official functions are held here.

In the days of old, the tsar's living quarters

**31.** *The Terem Palace.*
*The interior*

**32.** *The Palace*
*of Facets. The interior*

31

occupied the fourth floor of the TEREM PALACE. They consisted of five rooms following one another. A carved white-stone stairway leads to them. In olden times, it was known as the Golden Porch.

The first room of the Terem Palace was called the Front Hall or the Refectory; here boyars gathered every morning waiting for the tsar to appear. The second room, known as the Duma or Council Chamber, was where the tsar held conferences with boyars. The next one in turn, the Throne Room, served as the tsar's study. Only a few boyars enjoying the tsar's especial preference had access to this room. Adjoining it is the Royal Bedchamber connected with the Prayer Room, in there are two carved gilt cabinets housing a number of 17th- and 18th-century icons.

The original décor of the royal chambers has not survived. It is known that the wall paintings in the royal chambers were renovated almost every year. In the 1830s restoration work

was carried out in the palace. The wall paintings were executed in an "Old Russian" style sketches by Fyodor Solntsev, Academician of Painting. The windows were glazed with colour windowpanes and the tiled stoves were remodelled after old patterns.

The main façade of the PALACE OF FACETS (1487-1491, architects Marco Fryazin and Pietro Antonio Solari) looks out on to Cathedral Square. Adjoining its southern façade is the grand Krasnoye (Beautiful) Porch adorned with white-stone figures of lions, which was restored in 1994.

Its throne hall has an area of 500 square meters, which made it the largest hall in Moscow in its day, and is 9 meters high. Its groined vaults are supported by a massive central pillar, which is lavishly decorated with gilded white-stone carving showing dolphins, birds and animals. Important ceremonies and the sittings of the Zemsky Sobor, the National Assembly, were held here and foreign ambassadors were received in this hall. It was here in the Palace of Facets that Ivan the Terrible celebrated the capture of Kazan in 1552 and Peter the Great celebrated his victory in the Battle of Poltava.

The décor of the palace was changed more than once over the five centuries of its existence.

In 1882, the Belousov brothers, masters from Palekh (a village renowned for its distinctive paintings), reproduced the wall paintings in the hall according to a detailed description of the 16th-century subjects and compositions compiled by the noted Russian icon-painter Simon Ushakov. The paintings on the walls illustrate Biblical subjects and scenes from Russian history.

**35.** *West European silver articles dating from the 13th-19th centuries (Hall 5)*

**36.** *Ambassadors' gifts. Snow Leopard. London, England. 1600-1601*

36

35

**33.** *Old state regalia and ceremonial articles dating from the 13th-18th centuries (Hall 7)*

**34.** *Russian gold and silver articles dating from the 17th-early 20th centuries (Hall 2)*

THE ARMOURY, a world-famous museum and depository of unique cultural relics, is one of the oldest museums in Russia.

The present building of the Armoury was built by the St. Petersburg architect Konstantin Ton in 1851 specially for the museum.

The first written mention of the Moscow Kremlin's Armoury dates back to the year 1508. The Armoury contains exceptionally rich collections of masterpieces of 4th- to early

and wood carvers, metal chasers, jewellers, gold embroiderers, artists, and others—used to work. Most of them were talented folk craftsmen brought here from every part of Old Russia, including Vladimir, Suzdal, Novgorod, and other cities. Foreign masters were also invited to work here.

Exhibited in two of the Armoury halls are superb masterpieces by Russian gold and silversmiths from the 12th to the early 20th cen-

37

38

**37.** *Ceremonial*

*weapons. Detail*

**38.** *European armour*

*and weapons dating*

*from the 15th-19th*

*centuries*

20th-century Russian and foreign decorative and applied art. They include collections of articles made of precious metals, weapons and ceremonial horse attire, old royal regalia, ceremonial garments, and artistic embroidery produced at the workshops of the Moscow Kremlin's Armoury, the Royal Gold, Silver and Tsarina's Chambers, and the Stable Treasury, where not only armourers, but also skilful masters of various other specialities—metal, ivory

**41.** *Censer. 1598*

40

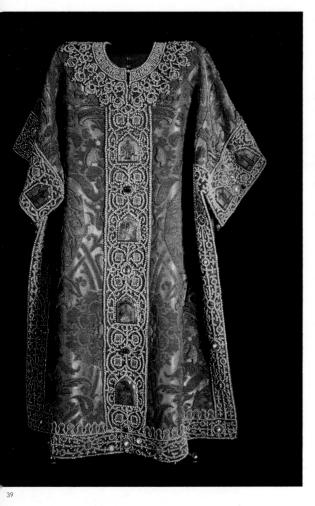

39

40

41

39. *Sakkos
of Patriarch Nikon.
The Moscow Kremlin
workshops. 1654*

40. *Sakkos
of Metropolitan Pyotr.
Russia. 1322*

turies: ladles, winecups, platters, vases, church plate, and icon casings.

The gold Gospel cover (1631-1632), which was intended as a donation to the Trinity-St. Sergy Monastery, was made by Gavrila Ovdokimov, the outstanding Moscow silversmith who worked at the Moscow Kremlin's Silver Chamber for more than forty years. He reproduced the composition of the Gospel cover dating from 1571. In his work, however, a tendency towards using intense colours is manifest: the precious stones and enamels are much brighter here and, besides, not only the filigree ornamentation, but also the architectural details are covered with colour enamels.

One part of the display is devoted to the celebrated firm of Peter Carl Fabergé famous for its jewellery articles of rare beauty. On show at the Armoury are its finest masterpieces—precious surprise Easter eggs.

Mikhail Perkhin, the talented jeweller, was

41

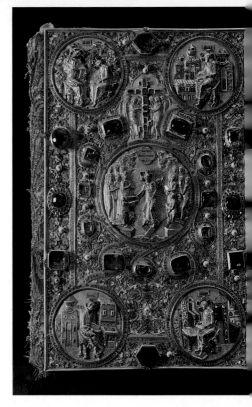

**43.** *The Gospel.*
*Moscow. 1st half*
*of the 17th century*

43

one of the firm's finest masters. In 1891, he made a miniature model of the cruiser Memory of Azov from gold and platinum on an aquamarine stand, placed inside a bloodstone egg. In 1899, the same master produced an exquisite gold clock in the shape of an egg, topped with a bouquet of lilies made of onyx. The little diamond hand of the clock is fixed and only its face made in the shape of a white enamel band turns around. The clock is a remarkable example of elegance and technical perfection.

The Armoury boasts a fine collection of 12th- to 19th-century weaponry. In this section are rare examples of military, ceremonial and hunting arms and knightly armour for the protection of both the rider and the horse, made by Russian, West European and Oriental masters. On display here are bows, quivers and arrows, suits of armour, coats of mail, sabres, swords, maces, spears, and battle-axes.

The display includes works by master armourers from Holland, Germany, England, Italy, and France. These are samples of jousting armour, cold steel, and firearms. The earliest exhibit in the collection is a 15th-century German set of armour distinguished by beauty and admirable proportion of all its parts. The elongated toes of its chausses covering the feet conformed to the shape of footwear that was in fashion at the time. Worn under such armour was a shirt of mail made of fine rings.

The Armoury also boasts a world-famous collection of 13th- to 19th-century West European silverware. The nucleus of the collection is composed of diplomatic gifts made by the heads of foreign states to the Russian royal house. The articles on display at the Armoury are works by silversmiths from Poland, Germany, England, Holland, France, Denmark, and Sweden.

The gifts of English ambassadors to Tsars Fyodor Ivanovich and Boris Godunov date from the period of transition from the Renaissance to the Baroque. They include two unique silver wine flagons in the shape of snow leopards with hinged heads serving as lids. The immense figures of the beasts standing on the hind legs are decorated with a fine linear repoussé pattern in imitation of the leopard coat. In their front paws the snow leopards hold shields ornamented with scrolls and leaves. Both these vessels were made in London in 1600-1601.

The Armoury display includes a collection

42. *Throne. Persia, before 1604. Presented to Tsar Boris Godunov by Shah Abbas I of Persia in 1604 (left)*

*Tsar Ivan the Terrible's Throne. Western Europe. 16th century (right)*

44. *The Cap of Monomakh. Late 13th-early 14th centuries*

43

of precious fabrics, Old Russian secular garments and sacerdotal vestments, 18th- to early 20th-century formal attire, and subject and ornamental embroidery.

The 18th-century ceremonial secular garments demonstrate that the style of the Russian and Western masters of the period had become rather similar. The Armoury collection includes a number of dresses made of rich patterned fabrics and adorned with precious lace and embroidery, including special dresses made for the coronation of the Russian empresses Catherine I, Anna Ioannovna, Elizabeth Petrovna, and Catherine the Great. Their skirts were stiffened and expanded by hoops of whalebone and their five metre long trains were borne on state occasions by ladies-in-waiting. Characteristic of these dresses is the heavy splendour of the Baroque style.

The earliest fabrics in the Armoury collec-

tion are those of Byzantine make. Byzantine satins ornamented with cross-shaped patterns were particularly highly valued in Old Russia. The sakkos (bishop's vestment) of light-blue satin with a pattern in the form of vertical gold stripes and crosses inside circles, made in 1322, used to belong to Metropolitan Pyotr, the first metropolitan of Moscow.

The collection of 13th- to 19th-century royal regalia and the tsars' court ceremonial articles is truly Russia's national pride. It has no equal among any of the European museum collections.

The first and best-known exhibit in this collection of masterpieces is the gold Cap of Monomakh made by an anonymous master in the early 14th century. It was used in the ceremony of crowning the Russian grand dukes and tsars down to Peter the Great. There exist quite a few legends about the origin and the name of the Cap of Monomakh. According to one of

**45.** *Carriages made in the 16th-18th centuries (Hall 9)*

them, the cap was given by the Byzantine emperor Constantine Monomachus, after whom it was named, to Prince Vladimir Monomakh of Kiev, his grandson, in the 12th century.

The older part of the cap is made of eight gold plates ornamented with a scrolled overlay of delicate gold filigree forming a pattern in the shape of six-pointed stars and a lotus flower. The hemispherical decoration with a cross on the top, the sable border and the pearls and jewels on the sides are later additions. The cap weighs 698 grams.

From 1762 on, the Russian emperors were crowned with the Great Imperial Diamond Crown, which is now on display at the Diamond Fund Exhibition. Nicholas II was the last Russian monarch to be crowned with this crown.

**46.** *Carriage of the Empress Elizabeth*
*Petrovna. France. 1757. Master Bournihalle*

46

**47.** *The coronation
dress of the Empress
Catherine I. Russia.
1724*

**48.** *Clock in the shape
of an Easter egg.
St. Petersburg,
Fabergé firm. 1899.
Master M. Perkhin*

The Great Imperial Crown, a true master
piece, was made by Jérémie Posier, the talented
court jeweller, for the coronation of the Empress
Catherine the Great in 1762. The crown consists
of two openwork hemispheres divided by a lush
floral garland and held together by a narrow cir
cular band. The cold glitter of the 5,000 dia
monds adorning the crown is offset by the dim
gleam of beautiful large pearls. The crown is
topped with a 398.72 carat noble spinel brought
to Russia by Nikolai Spafary, who was the Russ
ian ambassador to China in 1675-1678.

The Armoury collection of old royal thrones
is truly priceless.

In 1604, Shah Abbas I of Persia sent Tsar
Boris Godunov a throne in the form of a stool
with a low back of a traditional Oriental shape.
The throne is decorated with gold plates stud
ded with blue turquoise and red rubies.

The oldest one in the collection is Ivan the
Terrible's ivory throne. The wooden frame of

the throne is faced with carved ivory plates.

Also on show at the Armoury is a unique collection of 16th- to 18th-century carriages made by Russian craftsmen or purchased by the royal family in Europe. Each of them can be rightfully called a work of art.

The most beautiful royal equipage in the collection is the carriage presented to the Empress Elizabeth Petrovna by Count Kirill Razumovsky, Hetman of the Ukraine, in 1757.

This carriage was built of gilt carved maple by the French craftsman Bournihalle and decorated with pastoral scenes by painters from the school of the French master François Boucher. The pastoral scenes with cupids frolicking in the sky are placed in fancifully curved gilt frames.

The Armoury is a kind of an encyclopaedia of Russian history, where each exhibit is a true masterpiece of art.

49

**49.** *Russian state regalia: a crown, orb and sceptre.*
*The Diamond Fund Exhibition*

**50.** *Red Square* ▷

The Kazansky Cathedral in Red Square was built in 1630-1633 with money donated by Prince Dmitry Pozharsky in honour of the miracle-working Kazan Icon of the Mother of God. The cathedral, destroyed during the expansion of Red Square in the 1930s, has now been restored.

Similarly, the Voskresenskiye (Resurrection) Gates of the former Kitaigorod wall have been restored together with the chapel built specially for the Iberian Icon of the Mother of God—an exact copy of the miracle-working icon of the same name which is kept on Mount Athos in Greece.

In 1818, a monument to Citizen Minin and Prince Pozharsky (sculptor I. P. Martos), the heroes of the people's volunteer corps who were at the head of the Russian people's liberation struggle against foreign invaders in 1612, was put up in Red Square. It was built with money raised by public subscription.

**51.** *The Cathedral of the Kazan Icon of the Mother of God. Restored in 1993. Architects O. I. Zhurin and G.Ya. Mokeyev*

51

**52.** *The Voskresenskiye (Resurrection) Gates, also known as the Iverskiye Gates (after the Iberian Icon of the Mother of God). Restored in 1995. Architect O. I. Zhurin*

**53.** *Monument to Citizen Kuzma Minin and Prince Dmitry Pozharsky. 1804-1818. Sculptor I. P. Martos*

**54.** *The Cathedral of the Protecting Veil of the Mother of God (Cathedral of St. Vasily the Blessed). 1555-1561. Architects Barma and Postnik*

53

At the far end of Red Square opposite the Cathedral of St. Vasily the Blessed, stands the distinctive red-brick building decorated with turrets, ornamental patterns and numerous kokoshniki gables. It is the STATE HISTORY MUSEUM, built to the design of architect V. O. Sherwood and engineer A. A. Semyonov in 1874-1883.

The front façade of the building of the History Museum is consonant with the complex composition of the Cathedral of St. Vasily the

a long time it was the biggest commercial building in Moscow: its three long arcaded passageways cover an area of nearly 25,000 square metres.

The extended façade of the Upper Trading Arcades edges Red Square on its eastern side. Its large arched glass roofs over the rows of shops were long regarded as an unsurpassed achievement of engineering thought.

In the Alexandrovsky (Alexander's) Gardens by the Kremlin wall is the Tomb of the Unknown Soldier. Buried in this tomb are the remains of an unknown soldier, who was killed in action and buried in a common grave near the village of Kryukovo where the defenders of Moscow fought to the bitter end in 1941. The Eternal

**55.** *The State History Museum. 1874-1883. Architects V. O. Sherwood and A. P. Popov, engineer A. Semyonov*

**56.** *The Tomb of the Unknown Soldier*

**57.** *The grand entrance to the Alexandrovsky Gardens*

**58.** *The bowl-shaped fountain in the State Department Store (GUM)*

Blessed and the Kremlin and its slender turrets are reminiscent of the tent-roofed Kremlin towers. The building was designed and built in the traditions of 17th-century Russian architecture.

A beautiful bowl-shaped fountain is the compositional centre of the Upper Trading Arcades (now called the State Department Store, better known as GUM) built by architect Alexander Pomerantsev in the late 19th century. For quite

Flame keeps burning here in memory of those who fell during the Great Patriotic War of 1941-1945 and it lights up the inscription: "Your name is unknown, your feat is immortal."

The Alexandrovsky Gardens were laid along the western side of the Kremlin wall in 1820-1823. The wrought-iron gates of its grand entrance and its high fence were made to drawings by E. Pascal.

**59.** *The Upper Trading Arcades (now called the State Department Store, or GUM). 1889-1893. Architect A. N. Pomerantsev, engineer V. G. Shukhov*

**60.** *New public garden next to the Manège. Alexandrovsky Gardens*

In KITAIGOROD near the Kremlin is a street which is a veritable collection of masterpieces of old Russian architecture. It is called Varvarka Street after the Church of St. Barbara the Great Martyr, which is situated here.

In its architecture, this church was believed to be one of the finest in Kitaigorod. Originally it was built in 1514, during the reign of Grand Duke Vasily III, under the supervision of the Italian architect Aloisio with money donated by rich

the tavern you will see an old entrance hall, a large Official Chamber, and a cook-room (kitchen) with its own entrance hall and porch. The rooms of the lower floor were used as storerooms, cellars and butteries. The Official Chamber served as a formal reception room. This spacious chamber is covered by a brick vault supported by white-stone consoles. The exterior of the building is austere and laconic: its principal decoration is window openings

61

merchants Vasily Bobyor, Fyodor Vepr and Yushka Urvikhvostov, whose estates were situated nearby in the Zaryadye. Its present appearance took shape in 1796-1804 (architect R. R. Kazakov). The church, which is a first-rate example of Russian classical architecture, used to attract numerous believers by the miracle-working icon of St. Barbara the Great Martyr.

Situated next to the church is the Old English Tavern (16th-17th centuries). On entering

typical of 16th and early 17th century buildings.

In the 16th century, the mansion belonged to Ivan Bobrishchev, a rich merchant. After the historic Anglo-Russian trade agreement was concluded Tsar Ivan the Terrible granted Bobrishchev's mansion to the English. Subsequently, the English bought another mansion, in Ilyinka Street, and the one in Varvarka Street began to be called the Old English Tavern. When, in compliance with a royal ukase, the English had to leave Russia in 1649, the

ble and various modern materials. Its four twelve-storey buildings with an open inner courtyard in the middle form a rectangle and the central part of its northern wing is surmounted by a twenty-three-storey tower which offers a beautiful view of the Kremlin. It is, in effect, a kind of a housing project which has three restaurants, numerous cafés and bars, a two-hall Zaryadye Cinema (each hall seating 750), a concert hall seating 2,600, baths with a swimming-pool, a telephone exchange, and other facilities.

THE TRINITY CHURCH IN NIKITNIKI (1630-1650s) is a festive-looking "merchant" church shining with bright colours and presenting a variety of shapes. It was built in Nikitnikov Lane on commission from Grigory Nikitnikov, a rich merchant. Standing on a steep hill, the church could be seen from each side at the time when it was built.

62

63    64

mansion was sold to Boyar N. A. Miloslavsky. Subsequently it became the property of the Posolsky Prikaz (Foreign Office). Later on, it housed the podvorye (representation) of the Metropolitan of Nizhni Novgorod and in the reign of Peter the Great an Arithmetic School was opened in it.

THE ROSSIYA HOTEL (1958-1967, architect D. Chechulin and others) is built of concrete, steel, glass and iron and finished in white mar-

PUSHKIN SQUARE with its fountains, flowerbeds and old-fashioned street lamps is one of the most beautiful squares in Moscow. In the summer of 1880, a monument to Alexander Pushkin, the great Russian poet, was put up on the western side of the square at the end of Tverskoi Boulevard.

The monument was erected with funds raised by public subscription. Two competitions were held to choose the best design for the monument. As a result, the commission for the monument was given to A. M. Opekushin. The sculptor succeeded in creating a living image of the poet: Pushkin seems to have stopped for a few moments during a walk through an alley that he has frequently visited and now, lost in thought, his head inclined, is listening to a poem that is being born deep in his heart.

The ceremony of the unveiling, held on June 6, 1880, was attended by Ivan Turgenev, Alexander Ostrovsky, Fyodor Dostoyevsky, Alexei Pisemsky, Ivan Aksakov, and many other prominent figures of Russian literature and art. It was a great event in the life of the whole nation and a gala day for Russian literature.

In the 1950s, the monument was moved from Tverskoi Boulevard to Pushkin Square where it now stands.

65

*65. Monument to Alexander Pushkin. 1880. Sculptor A. M. Opekushin*

The Moscow City Hall building was built from the design by Matvei Kazakov in 1782-1784. It was then a three-storey mansion which, until the revolution of 1917, served as the residence of the governor general of Moscow. In October 1917 the building was taken over by the Central Military Revolutionary Council (the headquarters of the armed uprising in Moscow) and then by the Moscow City Soviet (City Council). Today it houses the offices of Moscow City Hall.

low relief. Adjoining the building on either side are gates with bronze grilles. Its intense red colour strikingly contrasts with the white-stone columns and gilding of its architectural décor.

Opposite the Moscow City Hall building lies Tverskaya Square. Here a monument to Prince Yuri Dolgoruky, the founder of Moscow, commissioned in 1947 to mark the 800th anniversary of Moscow (1147-1947), was unveiled on June 6, 1954. The monument was made from the design of sculptors

66

66. *Monument to Prince Yuri Dolgoruky and the building of the Moscow City Hall (formerly, the Moscow City Soviet building)*

In the years of Soviet rule the location and appearance of the building changed radically. In 1937-1938 it was moved back 14 metres to widen Tverskaya Street (known as Gorky Street at the time) and later on, in 1943-1945, two new storeys were added to it (design by architect D. N. Chechulin, with the participation of M. V. Posokhin and others).

In the centre of its façade the building has a two-tier portico with a pediment. The large arch of its entrance is decorated with sculptures in

S. M. Orlov, A. P. Antropov and N. L. Shtamm.

The monument shows Prince Yuri Dolgoruky riding a mighty charger. He is clad in a typical Old Russian suit of armour and a belted sword, with a shield adorned with the old emblem of Moscow. His right hand is reaching forth and with his left hand he is holding the bridle. The rider has a dignified and tranquil appearance and his glance and the motion of his hand seem to convey the idea, "A city will be founded here."

From every point in Teatralnaya Square one can see monumental white columns and above them, four rampant horses harnessed to Apollo's chariot. This is the building of the BOLSHOI THEATRE. In 1780, a public Petrovsky Theatre was opened on its site, but it burnt down in 1805. Nearly 20 years later, a new theatre was built in its place from the design of Osip Beauvais and Alexander Mikhailov. However, it shared the same fate: the theatre was greatly damaged by a fire in

Its magnificent ensemble consists of a main building with wings overlooking Mokhovaya Street and service buildings facing Starovagankovsky Lane. Standing on a high plinth, the central building is adorned with columns, statues, decorative vases, and wreaths and garlands moulded in stucco. In 1861, a Rumyantsev Museum, Moscow's first public museum and library, was housed in this building.

Opposite the Alexandrovsky Gardens behind

**67.** *The Bolshoi Theatre. 1821–1825. Architects O. I. Beauvais and A. A. Mikhailov*

1853. Its surviving walls and majestic eight-column white-stone portico were included in the new building erected by Albert Kavos in 1856.

On the crest of a low hill opposite the Kremlin stands the PASHKOV HOUSE, one of the most beautiful buildings in Moscow. The house was built in 1784-1786 supposedly by Vasily Bazhenov, the famous Russian architect, on commission from P. Ye. Pashkov, a rich Moscow nobleman.

a beautiful wrought-iron fence stands the old building of Moscow University (in Mokhovaya Street). Built from the design of Matvei Kazakov according to the austere principles of classicism, the building was restored after the fire of 1812 by Domenico Gilardi, who added features characteristic of the Moscow Empire style to its main façade. The décor includes sculptures in low relief, rosettes, and lion masks made to a sketch by sculptor G. T. Zamarayev.

68

69

**68.** *The Pashkov House.*
*1784–1788. Architect*
*V. I. Bazhenov*

**69.** *Moscow University*
*(old building).*
*1782–1793, architect*
*M. F. Kazakov;*
*1817, architect*
*D. I. Gilardi*

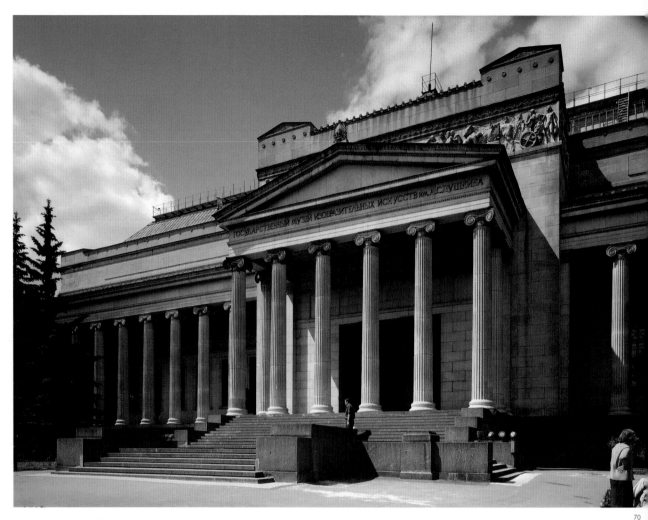

**70.** *The Pushkin
Museum of Fine Arts*

THE PUSHKIN MUSEUM OF FINE ARTS,
situated in Volkhonka Street in the old part of
Moscow, was built in 1898-1912 from the
design of the architect R. I. Klein.

Opened in 1912 under the auspices of
Moscow University, it was intended to be a public art education museum where everyone who
is fond of arts could get acquainted with the most
famous works of ancient, medieval and Renaissance art. Such were the goals set by its founder
Ivan Tsvetayev (1847-1913), Professor of Moscow
University, an outstanding expert in ancient
philology, who devoted his life to the task of setting up a museum of fine arts in Moscow.

Professor Tsvetayev oriented himself, in
the first place, towards museums of plaster
replicas that existed at universities in Berlin,
Paris and Dresden. When ordering plaster casts
abroad, he consulted with and followed the
advice of leading European and Russian experts
in history, archaeology and art.

Professor Tsvetayev organised a public
movement to raise funds for the construction
of the building and the purchase of exhibits
and became the founder of the museum. The
municipal authorities set aside a plot of land for
the project.

The construction of the museum was
financed mostly with private contributions. A
particularly generous contribution was made by
Yu. S. Nechayev-Maltsev, a prominent indus-
trialist who was the owner of a number of
glassworks.

The building of the Museum of Fine Arts
was laid down in 1898. The architect R. I.
Klein designed the building so that it would
house sculptures dating from different periods. The building is adorned with an Ionic
colonnade. On the façade above the entrance is
a sculptural composition by G. R. Zaleman on
the subject of the Olympic Games in Ancient
Greece. On the walls behind the columns on

60

either side of the main entrance is a frieze made of Tyrol marble by German sculptor L. Armbruster. It reproduced the frieze around the top of the wall of the Parthenon, the famous temple on the Acropolis in Athens built in the 5th century B. C., representing the Panathenaic procession of citizens honouring Athena.

On entering the museum you see a grand staircase leading to the halls on the first floor. The staircase is finished in several varieties of marble brought from Greece, Hungary and Belgium. The gallery above the staircase is surrounded with twenty monolithic columns of pink marble with bases and capitals of gilt bronze. The walls of the gallery are decorated with paintings on classical subjects by K. P. Stepanov and I. I. Nivinsky.

Initially, the museum's collections were composed mainly of plaster casts of sculptures dating from the 4th millennium B. C. through the Renaissance period. A plaster cast is an exact

71

72

**71.** *The grand staircase of the Pushkin Museum of Fine Arts*

**72.** *The hall of classical Roman art*

replica of the original, and so the museum's exceedingly rich collection of plaster casts is of great educational value. The collection includes plaster replicas of Ancient Greek and Roman and West European sculptural masterpieces the originals of which are far outside Russia. In the first few years of its existence the museum received a superb collection of Ancient Egyptian sculptures and works of applied art from V. S. Golenishchev, a prominent Egyptologist and a noted collector, as well as several paintings by 13th- and 14th-century Italian masters.

The museum's collection was considerably expanded in the 1920s when a number of private collections of West European paintings and sculptures, as well as the collection of paintings, engravings and drawings of the former Rumyantsev Museum and, later on, a number of first-rate originals from the Hermitage in Leningrad were handed over to the Museum of Fine Arts.

A new large department—a picture gallery featuring a fine collection of original works of 13th- to 20th-century West European painting—was opened at the museum. As a result, the museum turned from a depository of copies into a collection of original masterpieces. In 1937, to mark the 100th anniversary of Alexander Pushkin's death the museum was given the name of the great Russian poet.

The museum's collections, including its

and the Eastern Mediterranean, Ancient Greece and ancient Italy, Ancient Rome and the Northern Black Sea Coast in the classical period. The second section includes halls exhibiting plaster replicas of famous works of sculpture of the classical period, the Middle Ages and the Renaissance. The third section is a picture gallery where works of West European painting and sculpture from the Middle Ages to the present are on show.

73

**73.** *Nicolas Poussin.*
*Rinaldo and Armida*
*Late 1620s*

picture gallery, are constantly growing. Today it has about 5,000 paintings, 350,000 drawings and engravings, and 100,000 coins and medals. Its display gives you a clear idea of the development of world art from ancient times to our own day.

The museum's permanent display includes three main sections. The first one features original monuments of the ancient world—Ancient Egypt, the ancient civilisation of Anterior Asia

Here art lovers have a wonderful opportunity to admire canvasses by Rembrandt van Rijn, Peter Paul Rubens, Anthony Van Dyck, Sandro Botticelli, Bartolomé Esteban Murillo, and others. Of much interest is a collection of works by English painters such as John Constable, Thomas Lawrence, John Hoppner, and George Dawe.

The museum is particularly rich in French painting. Works dating from the 17th century

74. Pierre-Auguste Renoir.
*Portrait of the Actress
Jeanne Samary. 1877*

75. *Paul Gauguin. Queen
(King's Wife). 1896*

75

74

include paintings by Nicolas Poussin and landscapes by Claude Lorrain and Gaspard Dughet, and those dating from the 18th century include works by Jean Antoine Watteau, Jean-Baptiste Siméon Chardin, Jean Honoré Fragonard, and Jean Baptiste Greuze. Also on display here are works by Jacques Louis David, Jean Auguste Dominique Ingres, Théodore Géricault, Eugène Delacroix, Jean-François Millet, Gustave Courbet, Henri Rousseau, Charles-François Daubigny, Jules Dupré, Camille Corot, Paul Cézanne, Edouard Manet, Henri Matisse, Paul Gauguin, Pierre-Auguste Renoir, Edgar Degas, Vincent van Gogh, Pablo Picasso, and others. The museum's collections include original sculptures by Jean-Baptiste Lemoyne, Jean-Baptiste Pigalle, Jean-Antoine Houdon, and Clodion.

The museum, annually visited by more than 1,500,000 people, constantly holds exhibitions of paintings from the world's finest collections. On its part, it shows its collections at museums in Rome, New York, Paris, and other major cities of the world.

**76.** *The State Tretyakov
Gallery*

THE STATE TRETYAKOV GALLERY is a museum of world significance with collections running into many thousands of works of art, from Old Russian icons to contemporary paintings. The gallery is the pride of Moscow and all Russia.

Pavel Tretyakov (1832-1898), the founder of the gallery, began collecting the finest works by Russian painters in 1856 and continued his activity for forty years, until the end of his life. Works by Peredvizhniki (The Wanderers—Russian painters members of the Society of Wandering Exhibitions) featured very largely in his collection. The outstanding painters Ivan Kramskoi and Ilya Repin, the famous art critic Vladimir Stasov, and other prominent figures of Russian culture often took part in selecting pictures for the gallery. This made Tretyakov's collection a kind of a centre of artistic thought.

In the late 1860s, he began to collect works by painters of the first half of the 19th century and then, later on, works of 18th-century paint-

ing, which was little known at the time. Tretyakov was the first to appreciate the new trends in late 19th-century Russian painting and to begin buying works by young artists.

In the early 1880s, he built a gallery in Lavrushinsky Lane to house his collection of paintings. After Pavel Tretyakov's death, the building of the Tretyakov Gallery was expanded and decorated to sketches by the noted Russian artist Viktor Vasnetsov in the neo-Russian style, which better conformed to its purpose. The main façade of the gallery is a veritable fantasia on the themes of Old Russian architecture. Its shape and rich, festive-looking décor make the building reminiscent of an Old Russian palace. The right wing of the gallery was added later by the architect Alexei Shchusev.

The collector's brother, Sergei Tretyakov, also a lover of painting, collected works not only by Russian, but also by French and Dutch masters.

64

The collection of the Tretyakov brothers was opened to the public as a private museum in 1874 and it immediately became widely popular.

In 1892, after Sergei's death, Pavel Tretyakov added his brother's collection of paintings to his own and gave the gallery to the city of Moscow.

In the first half of the 20th century, the gallery was nationalised. Thus, formerly a municipal museum, the Tretyakov Gallery was transformed into a national museum. In the 1920s, the collections of I. S. Ostroukhov, I. Ye. Tsvetkov and S. A. Shcherbatov, noted Moscow art collectors, were given over to the gallery, as were paintings of the Russian school from the former Rumyantsev Museum, paintings previously kept at the History Museum, and works of art from various palaces, manors and churches. Besides, the gallery bought many works of art with funds allocated for the purpose by the government. Today it has about 47,000 works of art.

In the early 20th century, a department of Old Russian painting was instituted at the Tretyakov Gallery. It includes such great masterpieces as the famous Old Testament Trinity, the only original icon by Andrei Rublev, a number of other icons attributed to Andrei Rublev and Theophanes the Greek, and a collection of outstanding works of 16th-century Russian icon-painting.

76

77

78

*Andrei Rublev. The*
*...stle Paul. An icon*
*...the Deesis tier of an*
*...ostasis. Zvenigorod.*
*...y 15th century*

*Andrei Rublev. The*
*...hangel Michael. An*
*...from the Deesis tier*
*...n iconostasis.*
*...nigorod. Early 15th*
*...ury*

79

**79.** *Andrei Rublev. The Old Testament Trinity. 1st quarter of the 15th century*

The collection of 18th-century Russian art includes works by such talented portraitists as Alexei Antropov, Fyodor Rokotov, Dmitry Levitsky and Vladimir Borovikovsky and superb sculptural portraits by Fedot Shubin and Mikhail Kozlovsky.

The halls featuring the first half of the 19th century contain the remarkable canvas Christ's Appearance to the People by Alexander Ivanov, who devoted twenty years of his life to creating

it. On display here are also poetic yet true-to-life portraits by Orest Kiprensky, including his portrait of Alexander Pushkin, works by Karl Bryullov such as Bathsheba, A Lady on Horseback and a number of others, and genre paintings by Pavel Fedotov, each of which is an amusing account of an incident taken from life.

The next section of the gallery is devoted to the second half of the 19th century—the heyday of Russian realistic art. Paintings by Pered-

66

by Ivan Shishkin, moonlit nights, birch groves and steppes by Arkhip Kuinji, sunlit orchards and courtyards by Vasily Polenov, seascapes by Ivan Aivazovsky, and poetic paintings by Isaak Levitan conveying the artist's infatuation with the Russian scenery—have won worldwide recognition.

On display in the halls featuring Russian art of the late 19th and early 20th centuries are wonderful paintings by Repin's pupil Valentin Serov such as his Girl with Peaches, his portraits of the great actresses Glikeria Fedotova and Maria Yermolova, and others; canvasses by the talented painters Abram Arkhipov, Filipp Malyavin and Konstantin Korovin; historical paintings by Andrei Ryabushkin and Apollinary Vasnetsov; works by Alexander Benois, Konstantin Somov,

vizhniki constitute the most valuable possession of the Tretyakov Gallery. It boasts the biggest collection of works by Ilya Repin, including his paintings Ivan the Terrible and His Son Ivan on 16 November 1581, Unexpected Return, A Religious Procession in Kursk Gubernia, his portraits of Modest Mussorgsky and Lev Tolstoy, and others. Vasily Surikov, the great historical painter, is represented by such of his works as The Morning of the Streltsy's Execution, The Boyarina Morozova and Menshikov in Beryozovo. Paintings by Vasily Perov and Vasily Pukirev are filled with the bitter truth of life. Vasily Vereshchagin was one of the first in the world history of painting to show the seamy side of war and the sorrows and sufferings it brings. Profoundly psychological are portraits by Ivan Kramskoi, the leader of the Peredvizhniki group of painters, such as the portraits of Lev Tolstoy and Dmitry Grigorovich, his superb portrait of Pavel Tretyakov, the founder of gallery, and others.

Works by Russian landscapists—fields and country roads by Alexei Savrasov, dense forests

**80.** *V. A. Serov.*
*Portrait of O. F. Serova,*
*the artist's wife. 1895*

**81.** *M. A. Vrubel.*
*The Swan Princess.*
*1900*

82

Boris Kustodiev, and many others. Quite singular are paintings by Mikhail Vrubel—Pan, Seated Demon and The Swan Princess. Of much interest are also distinctive sculptures by Sergei Konyonkov and Anna Golubkina.

The extensive section of Russian art of the Soviet period boasts the finest works by masters of painting, sculpture and graphic art. The painters whose works are on show here include Mikhail Nesterov, Isaak Brodsky, Alexander Gerasimov, Arkady Plastov, Kukryniksy, and others, and the sculptors represented in this section include Vera Mukhina, Nikolai Andreyev, Ivan Shadr, and others.

Several years ago, a new status and a new official name, the All-Russia Museum Association "State Tretyakov Gallery," were conferred on the museum. Its old building in Lavrushinsky Lane has been reconstructed and expanded.

**82.** *I.I. Shishkin. In Countess Mordvinova's Forest. 1891*

**83.** *V. D. Polenov. A Moscow Side Street. 1878*

83

Members of the Moscow nobility built their mansions and palaces not only in the centre of Moscow, but also on its outskirts. These were country estates and out-of-town residences with beautiful parks, ponds and churches that belonged to the wealthiest men in Russia. Their owners went there to rest and hunt. There they gave balls, received distinguished guests and sometimes waited out periods of tsar's disfavour. These outskirts, most of which have retained their

In the 18th century, ceremonial receptions, grand gatherings and large-scale public festivities came into fashion, and Count Pyotr Sheremetev, the owner of the Kuskovo Estate, turned it into a "summer out-of-town pleasure home." He not only spent huge sums on the construction and decoration of his estate (from 1737 to 1785), but also proclaimed it open to the general public. Up to 25,000 people attended the festivities which he periodically held at Kuskovo.

**84.** *Panorama of the Kuskovo Estate from the direction of the pond*

names, have long become part of the capital. Many of them have been destroyed and lost forever under the onslaught of the great metropolis, yet quite a few of them have been preserved.

Today the finest of these estates and palaces are museums and areas protected by the state. They are exceedingly abundant in architectural monuments.

KUSKOVO—an outstanding 18th-century palace-and-park ensemble with a formal park noted for a strict geometric layout of alleys and neatly arranged rows of marble sculptures, ponds and reservoirs, a fanciful landscape garden, and majestic architecture—has aroused wonder and admiration among quite a few generations of lovers of the beautiful.

The names of several architects who took part in the construction of Kuskovo are to be found in Count Sheremetev's business correspondence with his stewards who administered the estate. They were Sheremetev's serfs Fyodor Argunov, Grigory Dikushin and Alexei Mironov, as well as hired freemen Yu. I. Kologrivov and Karl Blank. The name of the Parisian architect Charles de Vailly, under whom the famous Russian architect Vasily Bazhenov studied in his day, is also mentioned.

The main building of the estate, the Kuskovo Palace, was built on the bank of a large pond in 1769-1775 under the supervision of the Moscow architect Karl Blank from a design supposedly sent by Charles de Vailly from France. This single-storey wooden building is one of the finest examples of early classicism. Columns widely spaced in the centre afford ample room for a semicircular porch with sixteen steps. The central pediment of the palace is filled with ornate Baroque floral patterns in carved wood with Count Pyotr Sheremetev's Latin initials, PS.

The palace is the dominant architectural feature of the entire ensemble of the grand courtyard, which includes a church (1737-1739), kitchens (1755-1756, architect Fyodor Argunov), and a bell tower with a spire (1792, architects Alexei Mironov and Grigory Dikushin).

As was then the practice, the rooms in the palace are arranged in an enfilade: from the White Ballroom you may walk into the Card Room and then proceed to the Billiards Room, the Dining-room, and so on. Each room is originally and tastefully decorated and has its own purpose, colour and proportions.

The Crimson Room, called thus after the colour of the silk in which its walls and furniture are upholstered, has a particularly festive look. Everything in it—the parquet floor with a star-like pattern, the Baroque chandelier shining with its amethyst insets, the pendant crystals of the tall grand-looking girandoles on the walls, the set of 18th-century furniture on slender, elegantly

**85.** *The Grotto Pavilion and the Italian House*

**86.** *The Dutch House*

85

86

**87.** *A view of the pond from the direction of the Kuskovo Palace*

**88.** *The palace. The southern façade*

curved legs, and the mirrors in carved gilt frames—serves to emphasise its ceremonial character.

In the palace's ceremonial suites of rooms are paintings by noted Russian and foreign artists such as Ivan Argunov, Fyodor Rokotov, Georg Christoph Grooth, and N. B. Delapiere, sculptures by Fedot Shubin, articles of decorative and applied art, works by serf craftsmen, 17th- and 18th-century Flemish tapestries, patterned fabrics, mirrors, and crystal candleholders.

The enfilade of rooms ends with the immense White Ballroom. Its snow-white walls are edged with gilt baguette and pier glasses reflect the sparkling of crystal chandeliers. Its ceiling is dec-

**89.** *An alley in the park.*
*Kuskovo*

**90.** *K. A. Somov.*
*Lady Taking Off a Mask.*
*1906. Painted porcelain*

**91.** *I. P. Argunov.*
*Portrait of Kalmyk*
*Woman Anna*
*Nikolayevna. 1767*

**92.** *The palace. Private*
*dressing room*

**93.** *The palace's*
*southern enfilade*
*of staterooms*

orated with a large painted plafond and the floor is covered with beautiful patterned parquetry.

The windows of the White Ballroom give out on to a superbly laid out parterre of the formal park with decorative flowerbeds, fanciful fountains and marble statues. The park's main alley ends at the large building of the Conservatory (1761-1764)—a winter garden with a dance hall in the centre, built by Fyodor Argunov. To the left of the palace beside a small pond is another pavilion, the Dutch House (1749-1751), with a hipped tiled roof and beyond it is the Hermitage (1764-1767), an indispensable feature of every park at the time.

To the right of the parterre are another two pavilions—the Italian House (1754-1755) and the Grotto (1755-1765, architect Fyodor

89

Argunov, sculptural décor of the façades by M. I. Zimin, interior decoration by I. I. Vogt and others). The Grotto imitates an underwater cave—"Neptune's Kingdom." The walls and vaulted ceilings of its rooms are decorated with whimsical designs in the shape of mythical animals and fantastic plants made of shells, small pieces of coloured glass and illuminated limestone. The picturesque décor of the Grotto is enhanced by wrought-iron grilles on its windows and doors in the shape of seaweed.

In 1918, the Kuskovo Estate was given the status of a museum, which ensured preservation of its valuable possessions. In 1932, a Museum of Porcelain was opened here, which was subsequently transformed into a State Museum of Ceramics. It boasts an immensely rich collection

of Russian chinaware, from the first work by Dmitry Vinogradov, the founder of Russian china (1748) to works by contemporary Russian masters. Its section of foreign ceramics has collections of ancient pottery, Chinese, German, English,

90

91

French and Danish china and faience, majolica and glass. In 1938, the two museums were combined into one, the Kuskovo Estate-Museum (18th Century) and Museum of Ceramics.

94

OSTANKINO, a former estate of the Counts Sheremetev, is an architectural and artistic ensemble of the late 18th century.

The Princes Cherkassky, who owned Ostankino in the 17th and the first half of the 18th century, gave much attention to its development. Their wealth and noble rank and Ostankino's proximity to Moscow and the village of Alexeyevskoye, a tsar's residence, played not the least part in the development of the estate. The Church of the Life-Giving Trinity, built in 1678-1692 assumedly by master stonemason Pavel Potekhin, the Cherkasskys' serf, is the only structure that has survived since that time.

In the mid-18th century, the then suburban village of Ostankino passed into the ownership of the Sheremetevs. However, Pyotr Sheremetev, who was then busy building Kuskovo, paid little attention to Ostankino. It was only in the 1790s that his son, Count Nikolai

Sheremetev, an exceedingly wealthy man, a lover of the theatre and the owner of a superb company of serf actors, decided to build a palace-theatre on his estate. He invited a number of outstanding architects such as Francesco Camporesi, Giacomo Quareghi, and others to design the palace, but was not satisfied with the design and commissioned his own serf architects Alexei Mironov, Pavel Argunov and Grigory Dikushin, to do the job.

It took a decade to create the palace and park ensemble at Ostankino. During that period, the palace was built and its halls were decorated. Simultaneously with the palace, a beautiful park was laid out and a number of summerhouses and pavilions were built. There was no single plan of construction for the palace. Changes, additions and alterations were made during the construction of the Ostankino palace and its purpose was gradually expanded. In 1792, the building which only housed the

theatre was erected. In 1798, pavilions with connecting galleries and several halls—the Egyptian Pavilion intended for banquets and concerts, the Italian Pavilion for receptions, the Crimson Drawing-Room, the Blue Hall, and the Picture Gallery—were added to it. Thus, from a palace-theatre it was transformed into a palace of the arts, about which one of the contemporaries wrote: "In respect of splendour and magnificence, it has surpassed everything which the richest human imagination may offer or what the boldest fancy of an artist might picture."

The palace and park remember grand receptions and visits of crowned heads. At different times, the Emperors Paul I and Alexander I and King Stanislaw II August Poniatowski of Poland visited Ostankino.

Even by the yardstick of the splendid 19th century, the Ostankino Palace was quite outstanding in its luxury and a priceless collection of paintings, sculptures, and various rarities. Its rooms and halls were adorned with statues of Eros, Psyche, and other mythological personages. The Carpet Room was hung with expensive Gobelin tapestries and other rooms were decorated with beautiful chandeliers, elegant furniture and malachite tables.

Today the palace houses a Museum of Serf Art.

**94.** *The Ostankino palace of Count Sheremetev*

**95.** *Detail of the Italian Pavilion*

95

75

KOLOMENSKOYE, a former estate of the Moscow grand dukes and the Russian tsars, is situated on the high right-hand bank of the Moskva River. Today it is a museum-reserve, a monument of 16th- and 17th-century Russian architecture.

The village of Kolomenskoye was mentioned in Grand Duke Ivan Kalita'a will (1328) among his family estates. According to tradition, it was founded in the late 1230s by residents of Kolomna who had fled the town during the invasion of Khan Batu (1237-1238). Kolomenskoye always remained the "sovereign's possession," that is, it belonged first to the appanage princes and then the grand dukes of Moscow and later on, to the Russian tsars and emperors.

The birth in 1530 of Vasily III's son Ivan—the future Tsar Ivan the Terrible—was regarded at the time as an insurance of continuity of power and stability of the state. To mark the occasion, the Church of the Ascension was laid down as a symbol of the country's future glory. This tent-roofed church, noted for its rare beauty and proportion, is a superb monument

**96.** *The Church of the Ascension in Kolomenskoye. 1530–1532*

**97.** *Popular festivity in Kolomenskoye*

**98.** *The Church of St. John the Forerunner in the village of Dyakovo*

**99.** *The Bell-Tower Church of St. George. 16th century*

of 16th-century Russian architecture. It is not accidental that the church was described as a "wondrous wonder."

The main entrance to Kolomenskoye was through the stone Front Gates. In different years under the tsars of the Romanov dynasty the Water Tower (1640), the Dining Yard, the Regimental Chambers, the Kitchens, and other structures were built. In all, more than twenty architectural monuments have survived at Kolomenskoye.

On the grounds of the Kolomenskoye Museum-Reserve are a number of interesting samples of wooden buildings made in various regions of the country.

They include Peter the Great's house brought here from Arkhangelsk, the Entrance Tower of the St. Nicholas Monastery in Karelia (1691-1692), and others.

In the former village of Dyakovo, separated from Kolomenskoye by a deep gully, a Church of St. John the Forerunner consisting of five octagonal tower chapels on a single base was built in the mid-16th century.

Today Kolomenskoye is a favourite venue of popular festivities and theatrical shows featuring episodes from Russian history.

**100.** *The Petrovsky Stopover Palace*

**101.** *The Arkhangelskoye Estate. The manor house*

THE PETROVSKY STOPOVER PALACE has long been inside the circular boundary of the city of Moscow. It was built in 1775-1782 by the famous architect Matvei Kazakov on the grounds of a former Petrovsky (St. Peter) Monastery as an out-of-town royal residence where the tsars and tsarinas, who often travelled from St. Petersburg to Moscow, took rest before making a ceremonial entrance into the city.

At one time, there was a vast Petrovsky Park round the palace (today part of the park is occupied by the Dynamo Stadium).

Kazakov created a unique monument of 18th-century Russian architecture. The forms of the palace, which has a classicist overall composition, combine the Gothic and Old Russian style.

The main building of the palace, situated in the back of the grand courtyard, is the central feature of the architectural complex. It is topped with a magnificent dome on a massive drum cut through with arched kokoshniki gables and lancet windows.

The entrance into the palace was designed in the shape of a traditional Russian porch with columns. The service buildings and the brick fence with tall battlemented turrets lend the complex the appearance of a fortress. All its structures are built of dark brick and decorated with white stone and polychrome ceramics.

In September 1812, Napoleon, having left the Kremlin during the fire, spent several days in the palace. His army beating a retreat from Moscow plundered and devastated the building. It was only rebuilt in the 1830s under the supervision of Moscow architect I. T. Tamansky.

The Petrovsky Park, laid out round the palace in the 1830s, has survived to this day.

THE ARKHANGELSKOYE ESTATE-MUSEUM, formerly Prince Nikolai Yusupov's estate (from 1810), is a unique 18th-19th century palace-and-park ensemble.

The compositional centre of the Arkhangelskoye Estate is the palace, which was built here

back in the 1780s, in the days of N. A. Golitsyn, the grandson of Prince Dmitry Golitsyn, the original owner of the estate, by Russian serf architects according to a design by the Parisian architect Charles des Guerne.

The austere-looking two-storey palace, built in the 18th-century classicist style, is situated on the highest part of the estate. Its façade overlooking the park is adorned with a semi-circular colonnaded bay. The fine proportions of the palace are emphasised by a belvedere rising above its roof by 10.5 metres.

The palace is, in effect, a museum boasting a superb collection of paintings by famous artists such as Anthony Van Dyck, Giovanni Battista Tiepolo, François Boucher, Hubert Robert and others, as well as classical statues, fine furniture, mirrors, chandeliers, and articles of crystal and china.

The beauty of the park's alleys is enhanced by a number of elegant pavilions, summer-houses and fountains.

The park descends to the Moskva River in three picturesque terraces adorned with marble statues. In one of the alleys a bust of Alexander Pushkin, put up in memory of his visits to Arkhangelskoye, is to be seen.

THE FORMER TSARITSYNO ESTATE is situated in the southeast of Moscow. It is famous for its history, its architectural monuments and its remarkably beautiful scenery.

The first written mention of Tsaritsyno dates back to the late 16th century. At the time, it was a family estate of Tsarina Irina, the wife of Tsar Fyodor Ioannovich and the sister of Tsar Boris Godunov. The estate was then called Bogorodskoye. In the 17th century, Bogorod-

Bazhenov's designs for the empress and for her son Paul, the heir apparent, and his children, the half-finished Catherine's Palace, the Cavaliers' and Court Attendants' Buildings, the Opera House, the Fancy Bridge and a bridge over a gully, the Fancy Gates, and other structures have survived to this day.

These were structures built of stone and ornamented with white-stone lattice. The work was nearing completion when Catherine the

**102.** *The Bread Gates. The Tsaritsyno Estate*

**103-104.** *The Fancy Bridge. The Tsaritsyno Estate*

skoye was the property of the Boyars Streshnev and later on, of the Princes Golitsyn. In 1712, Bogorodskoye was renamed Chornaya Gryaz and Peter the Great gave it as a present to Moldavian Prince Sergei Kantemir, the father of Antiokh Kantemir, the noted poet and diplomat. Finally, in 1775, Catherine the Great bought the estate and called it Tsaritsyno Selo (Tsarina's Village). In the course of time this name was contracted to Tsaritsyno.

Catherine the Great commissioned the architect Vasily Bazhenov to design an ensemble of buildings for her out-of-town residence. She wished it to be built in a "Moorish-Gothic" style. Remains of the palatial buildings erected from

Great and her closest aide and favourite Prince Grigory Potemkin came to inspect the fanciful structures. The empress did not like the palace and ordered to tear it down. In 1786, Matvei Kazakov was commissioned to build a new palace. Its construction continued until 1793, yet the palace was left unfinished because of financial problems caused by the war with Turkey.

Since that time, a number of unfinished buildings that have suffered greatly from the ravages of time, magnificent picturesque ruins, the rather well preserved pavilions Milovida and Nerastankino, and the Ceres' Temple summerhouse have remained at Tsaritsyno.

THE NOVODEVICHY CONVENT, which at one time was Moscow's principal "guard" on its southwestern side, was founded in the early 16th century. This superb architectural monument is one of Russia's best-known cloisters.

The convent was built to commemorate the recapture in 1524 of the old Russian city of Smolensk. Founded by Grand Duke Vasily III, it was originally called the New Convent of the Smolensk Icon of the Mother of God "Hodegetria."

with twelve watchtowers. These walls checked the advance of the strong mounted force led by the Crimean Khan Kazy Girei when he attempted to capture Moscow in 1591. It was also here that Prince Dmitry Pozharsky won a victory over the troops led by Polish general Jan Karol Chodkiewicz in 1612.

In the 16th and 17th centuries, girls who were the daughters of the highest-born persons in the Russian state were admitted to the con-

**105.** *Panorama of the Novodevichy Convent from the direction of the pond*

It was a fortress convent guarding the road to Smolensk and Lithuania. And it was a major feudal institution: it was the owner of 36 villages in 27 uezds (districts) all over the country and in the mid-18th century it owned 15,000 male serfs.

The history of the convent is a fascinating chronicle where numerous examples of dramas and tragedies and of valour and humility are to be found.

The convent, built in a bend of the Moskva River, was surrounded with mighty walls topped

vent, and quite a few tsarinas and tsarevnas took the veil here. The widow of Tsarevich Ivan, the elder son of Tsar Ivan the Terrible whom he killed in a fit of rage, lived at the convent.

Tsarevnas and tsarinas, however, not always joined the convent of their own free will. In 1689, Peter the Great confined his sister Sophia in it following an abortive attempt to deprive her brother of the throne and, together with her, her three sisters—Catherine, Maria, and Theodosia.

**106.** *The Novodevichy Convent in winter*

**107.** *The watchtower and the over-the-gate Church of the Transfiguration. The Novodevichy Convent*

**109.** *Monuments and sculpted tombstones on the graves of prominent figures in Russian history and culture. The six-tiered bell tower (on the right). The Novodevichy Convent*

**111.** *The necropolis of famous Russian citizens in the Novodevichy Convent*

The convent was built mainly in the 16th and 17th centuries. Its oldest structure is the five-domed Cathedral of the Smolensk Icon of the Mother of God, built in 1524-1525. Its interior is decorated with frescoes depicting episodes of the struggle for a unified Russian state. In the late 17th century, Russian woodcarvers working under the supervision of masters Klim Mikhailov and Osip Andreyev, produced a multi-tier carved gilt iconostasis. In it, a number of works by Simon Ushakov, the outstanding 17th-century icon-painter, have survived.

The refectory, the bell tower and the churches standing next to the palatial chambers were all built in the 17th century as a single ensemble in the so-called Naryshkin Baroque style. Another feature common to all of the convent's main structures is their external décor—the festive-looking Old Moscow Baroque combining white-stone ornamentation and red-brick walls.

An exceptionally fine part of the complex is

the slender bell tower built in six octagonal tiers (1689-1690). Its gilt cupola can be seen from many parts of Moscow.

After the October 1917 revolution the convent was closed down, but the epidemic of demolition spared it. In 1922 the Novodevichy Convent was made into a museum and since 1934 it has been a branch of the History Museum. Today it is an acting convent.

Part of the convent's grounds is occupied by a necropolis where many prominent figures in Russian history and culture lie buried. Adjoining the convent is the Novodevichye Cemetery—an honorary burial ground where many of the country's noted personalities who left a noticeable trace in its history and contemporary life are buried. The tombstones that are to be seen here were executed in different periods by such famous sculptors as Nikolai Andreyev, Mikhail Anikushin, Yevgeny Vuchetich, Lev Kerbel, Sergei Konyonkov, Vera Mukhina, Nikolai Tomsky, Ivan Shadr, Leonid Sherwood, and others.

110

**108, 110.** *The Cathedral of the Smolensk Icon of the Mother of God in the Novodevichy Convent*

111

**112.** *The central nave of the Cathedral of the Smolensk Icon of the Mother of God*

**113.** *Inside the Cathedral of the Smolensk Icon of the Mother of God in the Novodevichy Convent*

**114.** *High-relief sculptures from the Cathedral of Christ the Saviour*

**115.** *The architectural ensemble of the Donskoi Monastery*

115

The Donskoi Monastery (Monastery of the Don Icon of the Mother of God) was founded in 1593 in memory of the salvation of Moscow in 1591 from an invasion by the hordes led by the Crimean Khan Kazy Girei at the spot where the Russian troops had pitched camp. Legend has it that a deserter defected to the khan and informed him that a great reinforcement from Pskov and Novgorod was about to arrive in Moscow. The khan decided to retreat, but the Russian troops ran him down and routed him.

By the yardstick of the day, the monastery was a mighty fortress surrounded with massive battlemented red-brick walls. The walls were topped with white-stone merlons, with twelve big round towers rising above them.

The Donskoi Monastery is a fine ensemble comprising a number of monuments of Russian architecture such as the Church of the Tikhvin Icon of the Mother of God (1713-1714, architect Ivan Zarudny [?]), a bell tower with the Church of Sts. Zacharias and Elizabeth (1730-1753, architects Domenico Tresini, Gottfried Johann Sch‰del, A. P. Yevlashov), the Church of the Don Icon of the Mother of God (1593, the "Old Cathedral"), the Cathedral of the Don Icon of the Mother of God (1684-1698, the "Big Cathedral"), and the Church of the Archangel Michael with the Princes Golitsyn's burial vault (1806-1809). The salient feature of the monastery complex is its compositional unity notwithstanding the fact that its structures were built in different periods and by different architects.

**116.** *The St. Daniel Monastery*

**117.** *The Trinity Church in the St. Daniel Monastery*

**118.** *Cathedral of Christ the Saviour. Designed by K. Thon. Reconstructed in the 1990s*

The recently restored ST. DANIEL MONAS-TERY is an official residence of the Patriarchs of Moscow and All Russia.

The monastery was founded on the right bank of the Moskva River in the late 13th century by Prince Daniil Alexandrovich, the founder of the dynasty of grand dukes of Moscow.

Some time after the death of Prince Daniil his son, Grand Duke Ivan Kalita of Moscow, transferred the monastery into the Kremlin. Later on, although the original monastery was on the decline, believers did not forget it thanks to rumours that passed around about cases of miraculous cure that occurred there.

Today the monastery has been completely restored and decorated with fine painting and rare icons.

119

120

THE CHURCH OF ST. SERGY OF RADO-
NEZH in Rogozhskaya Sloboda was built in
1796-1835. Its main altar is dedicated to the
Holy Trinity and its side chapels, to St. Sergy of
Radonezh and St. Nicholas the Miracle-Worker. In 1862, a new belfry was built in place of
the old tent-roofed one.

THE CHURCH OF ST. ELIJAH THE PRO-
PHET IN CHERKIZOVO (1690; rebuilt in
1883; belfry added in 1899) looks like an isle
of olden times amidst modern housing devel-
opments. In its iconostasis there are icons dating back to the 17th and 18th centuries.

**119.** *The Church of St. Sergy*
*of Radonezh in Rogozhskaya*
*Sloboda*

**120.** *The Church*
*of St. Elijah the Prophet*
*in Cherkizovo*

THE CATHEDRAL OF THE IMAGE OF OUR SAVIOUR "NOT-MADE-WITH-HANDS" (between 1410 and 1427) is one of the oldest surviving churches in Moscow. In its interior on the window scuncheons fragments of frescoes by the great icon-painter Andrei Rublev, who spent the last years here at the Monastery of Our Saviour built by St. Andronik as its monk, have survived.

THE STS. MARTHA AND MARY CHARITY HOUSE (1908-1912, architect A. V. Shchusev) is a small convent instituted initially as a charitable home for sick, wounded and disabled soldiers. It consists of several structures, including the cloister's main church, the Cathedral of the Protecting Veil of the Mother of God (1908-1912). In the cathedral's interiors subject and ornamental paintings by Mikhail Nesterov have survived.

**121.** *The Cathedral of the Image of Our Saviour "Not-Made-with-Hands." "The Monastery of Our Saviour built by St. Andronik*

**122.** *The Cathedral of the Protecting Veil of the Mother of God in the Sts. Martha and Mary Charity House*

121

122

**123.** *The Church of St. Nicholas the Miracle-Worker in Khamovniki. 1679–1683*

**124.** *The Church of the Icon of the Mother of God "Joy Unhoped-for" in Maryina Roshcha. 1903*

**125.** *The Church of St. Gregory Thaumaturgus in Bolshaya Polyanka Street. 1661–1679*

124

125

The estate CHURCH IN BYKOVO, built by Vasily Bazhenov in 1789 in the "Gothic style" vividly embodies the characteristic features of this style in Russian architecture. This church is considered to be unequalled in the originality of its spatial arrangement and in the elaboration of its individual shapes.

The church, faced in white stone, stands on a high crypt. Its western façade has twin belfry towers and an open grand staircase leading to its first floor. Its dome and belfries are topped with beautiful spires.

Its interior is decorated in the classicist style with the walls and columns finished in artificial marble. The belfries of the church were built in the mid-19th century.

The stone CHURCH OF ST. JOHN THE WARRIOR in Bolshaya Yakimanka Street (1709-1717) was built in keeping with the traditions of church architecture that were prevalent in its day, that is, in the form of a complex combining a church, a belfry, and a refectory. The Petrine period, however, had its effect on its design: the semicircular pediments at the centre of the walls and arcatures around its two lower tiers lend the church a festive look. In the eastern part of the refectory the church has

**127.** *The Church of St. John the Warrior*

*in Yakimanka Street*

**126.** *Bykovo. The estate church*

127

126

two side chapels dedicated to Sts. Gurias, Samonas and Abibus of Edessa and to St. Dimitry, Metropolitan of Rostov, marked with cupolas on the outside. In the church there are icons dating back to the 17th and 18th centuries.

THE CHURCH OF THE RESURRECTION IN KADASHI (old name of the district—Kadashevo; 1687-1713) is an outstanding monument of the Moscow Baroque style. The church was built with money collected by the inhabitants of Kadashevskaya Sloboda—weavers and artisans. A substantial sum of money was contributed by the Dobrynins, a wealthy merchant family. In 1860, the original church was considerably altered; it was then that it acquired its present appearance: a massive cube decorated with three rows of openwork white-stone fes-

toons. Twin columns on the façade at the corners of the cube, platbands with wreathed
columns over its windows, and rich, exquisite
white-stone carving make this church one of the
most beautiful in the Zamoskvorechye.

THE CHURCH OF THE PROTECTING VEIL
OF THE MOTHER OF GOD in Fili was built
in 1690-1694 with money donated by Lev
Naryshkin, Peter the Great's uncle. It is another fine example of the Moscow (Naryshkin)
Baroque style. This elegant, well-proportioned
church stands on a high terrace. The church is
made in five tiers with broad grand staircases
leading to its first floor

**128.** *The Church*

*of the Resurrection in Kadashi*

**129.** *The Church of the Protecting*
*Veil of the Mother of God in Fili*

128

129

THE KUZMINKI ESTATE was founded by A. G. Stroganov in the early 18th century and later, between 1820 and 1917, it was the property of the Princes Golitsyn. Taking part in building the estate complex were architects Domenico Gilardi, I. V. Yegotov, and S. A. Toropov.

The Church of the Blachernae Icon of the Mother of God (1759-1762, 1774, architect I. P. Zherebtsov; rebuilt in 1794-1798 by architect R. R. Kazakov) was originally designed in the

wrought-iron grilles, bollards with chains, and hanging bridges over gullies and streams made at S. M. Golitsyn's works in the Urals. What has survived in Kuzminki offers a good idea of how beautiful this palace-and-park ensemble once was. Particularly grand-looking was the entrance to its ceremonial courtyard—elegant wrought-iron gates flanked with street lamps that were decorated with sculptures of griffins and lions. Today the estate is one of the Mus-

**130.** *The Kuzminki Estate*

**131.** *The Trinity Church in Troitskoye-Golenishchevo*

Baroque style and completed in the classicist style.

The splendid Stable Yard (1819-1823) with a Music Pavilion adorned with a sculptural group featuring Apollo and the Muses at the centre of its façade has survived. Leading to it is a broad staircase, which was decorated in 1847 with cast metal copies of the equestrian sculptures by the noted sculptor Pyotr Klodt (1841) adorning the Anichkov Bridge in St. Petersburg. The pavilion burnt down in 1978 and now it has been built anew.

In the estate park there were numerous

covites' favourite recreation haunts.

Situated between the Poklonnaya Hill and the Vorobyovy Hills was the village of Troitskoye-Golenishchevo, a summer residence of the Metropolitans and Patriarchs of All Russia. Here on a hillside a remarkable tent-roofed stone TRINITY CHURCH has survived. The church was built in 1644-1646 by master stonemason Larion Ushakov from the design of Antip Konstantinov. Besides the main building, the church has two symmetrical side chapels, each covered with a tent roof.

N. VTOROV'S MANSION (1913-1914, architects V. D. Adamovich and V. M. Mayat) with twin columns, and open half-rotunda, recessed windows, and a large semicircular window with figures of flying glory goddesses in low relief above it is a perfect example of the Empire style

The mansion is rented by the United States Embassy to Moscow.

In its composition, I. G. KHARITONENKO'S MANSION (1891-1893, architect D. N. Chi-

first-floor side windows are male busts.

This beautiful building on Sofiiskaya Embankment opposite the Kremlin houses the Embassy of the United Kingdom.

The three-storey red building of THE ENGLISH CLUB (1811, architect A. A. Menelas [?]; 1814-1817, architect D. I. Gilardi [?]) with an eight-column portico is separated from Tverskaya Street by a beautiful wrought-iron fence

**132.** *N.Vtorov's mansion*

chagov with the participation of F. O. Shekhtel) with service buildings is reminiscent of a typical town estate of the classicist period of the late 18th-early 19th centuries with a large ceremonial courtyard behind a beautiful wrought-iron figured fence with two gates on its sides on Sofiiskaya Embankment. In the centre of the main building's façade is the entrance covered with a beautiful canopy supported by four columns, which doubles as a wide first-floor balcony. Above the gauged pediments of the

with stone lions. Since 1924, this building has housed the Museum of the Revolution.

The mansion was built in the 1780s by Mikhail Kheraskov, the noted Russian poet. After 1812, the mansion became the property of Count Razumovsky, who rebuilt it in the classicist style. From 1831, the building housed the aristocratic English Club.

In the late 19th-early 20th centuries, the building was subjected to some minor alterations; later on, however, it was restored to its former shape.

**133.** *The mansion of I. G. Kharitonenko (P. I. Kharitonenko)*

**134.** *The English Club in Tverskaya Street (K. L. Razumovsky's mansion; now housing the Museum of the Revolution)*

133

134

In 1889-1893, a distinctive-looking mansion was built for the family of the MERCHANT IGUMNOV. The architect N. I. Pozdeyev was requested to build a house in the Old Russian style that would be comfortable enough for modern living. The architect modelled his design after 17th-century wooden houses and built a stylised mansion. This found expression in the shape of the porch, the windows, and many of the details of its exterior décor. Its architectural shapes, in cation, just as the shapes of the structure were suggested to the architect, who had been born and raised in the city of Yaroslavl, by medieval Yaroslavl architecture. Besides ceramics, wood and white-stone carving, wrought and cast metal ornamentation and patterned brickwork were used in decorating the mansion. The polychrome tiles and carved white-stone ornaments lent the mansion a particularly festive look. Apparently, that was late 19th-century Muscovites' idea of

135

**135.** *N.V. Igumnov's mansion in Bolshaya Yakimanka Street*

**136.** *The grand staircase in N.V. Igumnov's mansion*

particular, its barrel-shaped roof with tent-like projections and its porch with hanging tie-pieces, and its Old Russian ornamentation made it look rather like a stage set.

The décor of the façades of this unique structure includes a great number of polychrome tiles, imitating 17th-century Russian tiles, made at M. S. Kuznetsov's works to drawings by M. S. Maslennikov. The lavish use of ceramic decoration, its ingenious yet strictly traditional appli-

Old Russian wooden and stone houses.

The interiors of the house, lavishly decorated with painting and stucco moulding, are also reminiscent of an Old Russian mansion.

Today Igumnov's mansion houses the Embassy of the French Republic. The embassy has built a new, modern building next to it, since a merchant's house, while being quite suitable for holding formal receptions, hardly conforms to the status of an official diplomatic mission.

**137.** *The building
of the Trusteeship Council*

**138.** *The Lunins'
house.
Architect D. I. Gilardi.
1818–1823*

The building of THE TRUSTEESHIP COUNCIL (now housing the Russian Academy of Medical Sciences) in Solyanka Street and the Lunins' house in Nikitsky Boulevard, built in the first quarter of the 19th century, are superb examples of the Empire style, which are among the finest works by the outstanding architect Domenico Gilardi.

Originally the Trusteeship Council complex consisted of three separate buildings—the main building and two side wings linked by a stone fence with entrance gates. In 1846, two-storey buildings (architect M. D. Bykovsky) were erected in place of the fence. They connected the three buildings into one. Above an eight-column portico there is a small dome. The stucco moulding in low relief and the friezes on the façade are by the sculptor Ivan Vitali.

THE LUNINS' HOUSE has a large iron balcony with an elegant wrought-iron railing. The stucco moulding decorations on the plain walls of the façade include representations of musical instruments in honour of the wife of the master of the house, who was a talented singer.

Going up the Sretensky Hill beyond Trubnaya Square is Rozhdestvensky Boulevard. This place has been known since the late 14th century when the Rozhdestvensky (Nativity of the Virgin) Convent after the boulevard was named was built here on an elevation along the course of the Neglinnaya River.

THE FORMER ALEXANDROVSKY (ALEXANDER'S) INSTITUTE (now the Institute of Tuberculosis) was built in 1809-1811 from the design of Domenico Gilardi. Originally the complex was intended for accommodating a Widows' Home. Later on, the building housed the Alexandrovsky Institute for Children of Impoverished Gentry and Commons, one of the first educational establishments for women in Russia.

In the centre of its façade is a majestic Corinthian portico topped with a pediment, standing above the arcade of the main entrance.

Situated next to it, at 2 Dostoyevsky Street, is the building of the Mariinskaya Hospital (1803-1805). Its eastern wing where Fyodor Dostoyevsky, the world-famous writer, was born in the family of a doctor on October 30, 1821, now houses the Dostoyevsky Museum.

139

**139.** *Rozhdestvensky Boulevard*

**140.** *The Alexandrovsky Institute. Architect D. I. Gilardi. 1809–1811*

140

141

N. I. MINDOVSKY'S MANSION in Prechis-
tensky Lane is one of the earliest examples of
the Moscow neo-classicist style. Its three-part
composition with different façades is united
by an magnificent corner rotunda with twin
columns. The mansion was built in 1906 to the
design of architect H. G. Lazarev.

THE TCHAIKOVSKY CONCERT HALL
(1940, architects D. N. Chechulin and K. K.
Orlov) is one of the centres of Moscow's musical and cultural life. Its auditorium, arranged in
an immense three-tier amphitheatre, has excellent acoustics and a very convenient layout so
that a spectator occupying any seat has a full
view of the stage.

THE TCHAIKOVSKY MOSCOW CONSER-
VATORY is a late 18th century manor house
built to the design of Vasily Bazhenov (?) for
Princess Yekaterina Dashkova. In 1894, the
building was almost entirely torn down. In
1901, architect V. P. Zagorsky rebuilt the building so that it could house the conservatory,
using elements of Dashkova's manor.

The Great Hall of the Moscow Conservatory, equipped with a great organ, is noted for
its superb acoustics achieved by using a sys-
tem of hollow ceramic vessels built into its

142

143

ceiling. On the walls of the auditorium are medallions with portraits of Russian and foreign composers—Tchaikovsky, Glinka, Beethoven, Wagner, Bach, Handel, Mozart, Schumann, and others. Here on the stage of the Great Hall concerts of symphony and chamber music are given, the finest musicians perform and the Tchaikovsky International Competitions of pianists, violinists and vocalists are held.

In 1954, a monument to the great Russian composer Pyotr Ilyich Tchaikovsky (sculptor Vera Mukhina) was put up in front of the Conservatory building. On the railings at the foot of the monument there are fragments of music from the composer's works.

**141.** *N. I. Mindovsky's mansion*

**142.** *The Tchaikovsky Concert Hall*

**143.** *The Great Hall of the Moscow Conservatory*

**144.** *The monument to P. I. Tchaikovsky in front of the building of the Moscow Conservatory*

**145.** *The Tchaikovsky Conservatory (Ye. R. Dashkova's house)*

**146.** *The Metropole Hotel*

THE METROPOLE HOTEL, one of the best in Moscow, was built in 1899-1903 to the design of William Walcott, a Moscow architect of Scottish origin, in the Art Nouveau style.

The upper part of its façade is adorned with decorative majolica panels. The largest of them, which is on the wall facing Neglinnaya Street, was designed by the celebrated artist Mikhail Vrubel on the theme of the play La Princesse lointaine by the French playwright Edmond Rostand. The rest of the compositions include Veneration of the Deity, Veneration of Nature, Life, and other pieces made to sketches by Alexander Golovin.

A. I. DEROZHINSKAYA'S MANSION in Kropotkinsky Lane (former Shtatny Lane) and S. P. Ryabushinsky's mansion in Malaya Nikitskaya Street were built at the same time, in 1900-1904, to designs by architect Fyodor Shekhtel in the Art Nouveau style.

Ambiguity of division into storeys, large

**147.** *Decorative panel made from drawings by M. Vrubel. The Metropole Hotel*

106

**148.**

*A. I. Derozhinskaya's mansion in Shtatny Lane (13 Kropotkinsky Lane)*

**149.**

*S. P. Ryabushinsky's mansion in Malaya Nikitskaya Street*

windows, preference given to curved lines, the use of mosaics are some of the features which distinguish houses built by Shekhtel from nearly identical mansions put up in the late 19th-early 20th centuries. The mansions that he designed were surrounded with wrought-iron railings in the shape of a spiral of some other fanciful pattern symbolising his desire to get rid of traditional fences.

Today S. P. RYABUSHINSKY'S MANSION houses a museum of A. M. Gorky, the great Russian writer who lived here from 1931 to 1936.

148

149

Z. G. MOROZOVA'S MANSION in Spiridonovka Street is one of the first major works by the noted Russian architect Fyodor Shekhtel (1859-1926). The architecture of the mansion, built in 1893-1898 on commission from Savva Morozov, combines Gothic and Moorish motifs treated in keeping with the principles of the Art Nouveau style.

The building was deliberately made to look monumental. When you approach the man-

griffins, chimeras—who seem to be growing out of architectural decorative shapes and, forming a kind of 'fourth dimension,' are living their own lives." (Ye. A. Borisova and G. Yu. Sternin)

Leading to the anteroom is a grand staircase with wooden banisters and in its back is a transparent "Gothic" stained-glass window. At the entrance to the grand staircase is the sculptural group Robert and the Nuns by Mikhail Vrubel. One of the drawing-rooms in the man-

150

**150.** *Z. G. Morozova's mansion in Spiridonovka Street. The garden façade*

**151.** *The anteroom in Z. G. Morozova's mansion in Spiridonovka Street*

sion on the outside or find yourself inside its ceremonial interiors, it seems to be bigger than it really is.

"This private mansion in an old Moscow street looks like a mysterious, otherworldly, magic castle out of Perrault's fairytales, inhabited by giants and other fantastic beings rather than real people. The ceremonial interiors of Z. G. Morozova's mansion are veritably 'overpopulated' with unreal personages—dragons,

sion is adorned with three decorative panels—Morning, Noon, and Evening—by this celebrated artist.

Later on, the mansion became the property of M. P. Ryabushinsky and on his commission in 1912 artist K. F. Bogayevsky produced three landscape panels for one the mansion's drawing-rooms. "Exotic landscapes with fantastic plants seem to be opening to the outside, into another world, the space of a comparatively

152

153

small room, making it boundless, going to infinity, blurring the clear-cut outlines of the walls and the strictly geometrical shape of the drawing-room." (Ye. A. Borisova and G. Yu. Sternin)

In 1995, its interiors were badly damaged by a fire. The building, which is now a reception house of the Russian Ministry of Foreign Affairs, is being restored. Some 70 percent of wood carving, gilt stucco moulding, sculptures and stained-glass windows were lost in the fire. And yet today this veritable treasure house has risen anew from the ashes.

**152.** *The drawing-room with a panel by K. F. Bogayevsky in Z. G. Morozova's mansion in Spiridonovka Street*

**153.** *The dining-room in Z. G. Morozova's mansion in Spiridonovka Street*

154

**154.** *The grand staircase in Z. G. Morozova's mansion in Spiridonovka Street. Robert and the Nuns. Sculptural group by M. A. Vrubel. 1896—1898. Bronze*

Prechistenskaya Embankment stretches along the left bank of the Moskva River from Soimonovsky Passage to the Crimean Bridge. Here a house was built in the late 19th century on commission from I. Ye. Tsvetkov, a noted Moscow collector of Russian painting, specially for a picture gallery which he, together with his house, gave to the city of Moscow in 1903.

century Russian architecture—platbands round the windows, polychrome tile panels, etc.

In 1905-1907, architect N. K. Zhukov built a stone house in a Russian fairytale style for merchant P. N. Pertsov. Built on the corner of Soimonovsky Passage next to Tsvetkov's house, it is decorated with parti-coloured majolica panels featuring themes from an old pagan epic

Initially (1899) the design was developed by architect L. N. Kekushev, but it never materialised. Some of its features such as an immense barrel-shaped roof were subsequently used by the artist Viktor Vasnetsov from sketch the house was built by architect B. L. Schnaubert. The small two-storey building of the gallery is reminiscent of a casket lavishly decorated with somewhat modernised elements of 17th-

and other ceramic insets produced by the Murava artel of potter artists from sketches by the painter Sergei Malyutin. Malyutin designed not only the building's façades, but also some of its interiors. Part of the décor of the main staircase and some of the elements of interior decoration in the flats have survived.

**155.** *P. N. Pertsov's house
on Prechistenskaya Embankment*

**156.** *The Central
Architects' House
in Granatny Lane*

**157.** *I.Ye. Tsvetkov's house*

157

THE CENTRAL FAÇADE OF THE CENTRAL ARCHITECTS' HOUSE (1939-1941) was designed by A. K. Burov. The façade is in the form of an add-on three-arch portal the wall of which is faced with dark-red matted ceramic tiles. Light-grey marble, golden smalt and artificial white stone were also used in decorating the façade. The overlaid majolica cartouche representing the master plan of the development of Moscow is by the artist Vladimir Favorsky.

The housing development known among the Muscovites as the "HOUSE ON THE EMBANKMENT" after the title of a novel by the noted writer Yuri Trifonov was built to the design of the noted architect Boris Iofan in 1928-1931 as a residential complex for the Central Executive Committee and the Council of People's Commissars (governmental bodies of the period). This immense structure extends from Bersenevskaya Embankment to the drainage canal. Its buildings, grouped round three well-groomed courtyards, combine housing for a total of 500 flats and service facilities such as sports facilities, schools, a department store, a canteen, and a community centre. It also includes, as separate units, the Udarnik Cinema and the Variety Theatre.

159

The new buildings of THE RUSSIAN STATE LIBRARY were erected next to its former building, the Pashkov House. They were built in 1927-1941 from the design of architects V. Shchuko and V. Gelfreikh.

The book repository building, situated in Starovagankovsky Lane, is parallel to the reading-

**159.** *The residential complex of the Central Executive Committee and the Council of People's Commissars with a department store and the Variety Theatre ("House on the Embankment")*

**158.** *The Russian State Library*

158

rooms building in Mokhovaya Street. At the corner of Mokhovaya and Vozdvizhenka Streets is a spacious terrace with grand staircases leading to the main entrance. The terrace is bordered on three sides by propylaea with tall square columns faced with dark marble. The buildings are decorated with sculptural pieces: above the pylons of the façade overlooking Mokhovaya Street there are 14 allegorical statues, and in the niches there are bronze portraits of great writers and scientists of the world. The main portico is topped with a multi-figure frieze in relief.

The "wedding-cake" skyscraper—a tall building in a style popularly known as Stalinist classi-

glorify labour, maternity, and learning.

In Moscow, buildings having more than 26 storeys are regarded as tall. Seven such buildings were erected in the late 1940s and early 1950s in compliance with a special resolution of the Council of Ministers adopted in 1947. The sites for them were selected on elevations, the "seven

**160.** *A sculpture and a low relief adorning a "wedding-cake" skyscraper*

**161.** *A side building of the "wedding-cake" skyscraper in Kudrinskaya Square*

160

161

cism – on the western side of Kudrinskaya Square was built to the design of architects M. V. Posokhin and A. A. Mndoyants in 1954. It is a residential complex which also includes shops and a cinema in the stylobate. The structure has a three-part composition consisting of a tall central tower and two 8- and 17-storey stepped side buildings. The central 22-storey volume, topped with an octagonal spire, is 156 metres high. The whole structure stands on a relatively low stylobate, faced with granite, on top of which are promenade terraces. The sculptures and bas-reliefs decorating the skyscraper

Moscow hills," in order to emphasise the natural features of the terrain and the radial-circular structure of the city plan. In constructing the buildings, sophisticated reinforced concrete and steel post-and-beam framing were used.

The tall buildings were intended for Moscow University, a palace for science and young people; the Ministries of Foreign Affairs and Foreign Trade; an office and residential building in Lermontovskaya Square; residential complexes in Kudrinskaya Square and on Kotelnicheskaya Embankment; and the Ukraine and Leningradskaya hotels.

BRIDGES ACROSS THE MOSKVA RIVER have always been among the city's attractions. At first, narrow wooden and then, later on, stone and welded metal ones, they not only linked different districts of the capital, but also became major landmarks in its history.

THE CRIMEAN BRIDGE was built in 1938 from the design of engineer B. P. Konstantinov and architect A. V. Vlasov. The Moskva River is shallow here and in olden times this part of it was known as the Crimean Ford, over which Crimean Tatars crossed the river during their raids on Moscow. There was a great deal of traffic over this area, and in 1785 the wooden Nikolsky Bridge was built here. Ninety years later, in 1873, it was replaced by an iron bridge with lattice girders. The bridge was narrow and congested with traffic. In 1937, a new, modern Crimean Bridge was built in its place. The bridge together with the approaches is 671 metres long and 33.3 metres wide. The whole structure looks light and graceful and seems to be hanging in midair.

THE BORODINSKY BRIDGE was built in 1911-1913 to mark the 100th anniversary of the famous Battle of Borodino between the Russian army

**162.** *The Crimean Bridge*

162

163

and Napoleon's Grande Armée (1812). The bridge was erected at the beginning of the Mozhaisk Highway leading to the site of the battle in place of the old Dorogomilovsky Bridge (1787-1788), which was called the Borodinsky Bridge from 1847.

The authors of the design—engineer N. I. Oskolkov and architect R. I. Klein—decorated the bridge in a solemn, triumphal manner. On the side of Smolenskaya Square the bridge opens with

In days of old, Moscow suffered greatly from floods through the overflowing of the Moskva River. Sometimes strong springtime freshets swept away whole neighbourhoods of wooden houses standing on the low left-hand bank of the river. Finally, in the late 18th century the first embankments were built on the banks of the Moskva River so as, on the one hand, to restrain its quick temper and, on the other, to make the banks of the river more convenient for living and running

**163.** *The Borodinsky Bridge*

**164.** *The Moskva River by night*

propylaea featuring stone Doric columns, which are supplemented with cast-iron and bronze décor. The pylons are topped with exquisite compositions in the form of ancient military armour; the frieze of the colonnades includes finely shaped laurel wreaths; the decorative railings of the bridge are ornamented with insets made to look like Roman shields. Also put up on the bridge are bronze memorial plaques bearing the names of heroes of the Patriotic War of 1812.

transport facilities. In the early 1790s, the wooden embankments were replaced with stone ones and subsequently, in the late 18th and early 19th centuries, stone piers were added to some of the embankments. Descents leading to the river were made for horse-drawn vehicles and water carriers.

Today the length of embankments in Moscow has reached 100 kilometres. Almost all of them are faced with granite and have motor roads running along them.

In 1956, the UKRAINE HOTEL, one of the biggest in Moscow, was built in a bend of the Moskva River at the beginning of Kutuzovsky Prospekt. Besides 1,000 guest rooms, a restaurant and a café, the complex includes a residential section with 254 flats and its street-level part houses several shops. The building, including the spire, is 170 metre high. Its central tall tower has 29 storeys.

165

166

167

Classical pyramidal obelisks topping the tiers of the building alternate with ornamental attics featuring five-pointed stars and vases in the form of sheaves of wheat. The towers of the side wings are topped with monumental sheaf-like vases symbolising the fertility of the Ukrainian land—a well-known producer of grain.

In front of the hotel's main entrance facing the embankment there is a small public garden in the centre of which stands a monument to the Ukrainian poet Taras Shevchenko. The architectural ensemble of the hotel was designed by A. G. Mordvinov, V. K. Oltarzhevsky and V. G. Kalish.

**165.** *The Borodinsky Bridge*

**166.** *Moscow by night*

**167, 168.** *The Ukraine Hotel*

The blue ribbon of the Moskva River flowing through the Russian capital rises in a marshy area in the Smolensk-Moscow Upland. Having passed some 320 kilometres, the river enters the city near Tushino, then on its way through the city it makes three round bends, moving towards the southeast, and leaves the city limits at Kapotnya. Finally, near the town of Kolomna, it flows into the Oka River. The length of the river within the limits of the city is more than 90 kilome-

men making cauldrons used to live (its mention dates back to the year 1632). The river bank was for them a backyard where every kind of garbage was discarded. The Moskva River was then flowing within its natural banks and there was no traffic along them. It is hard to imagine that all you could see here in the last century was impassable mire and mud on a littery bank by which you could not approach the river nor get onto land from the river.

**169.** *Kotelnicheskaya Embankment*

tres and its width reaches 200 metres in some places. The ribbon of the Moskva River with its bends, picturesque banks, broad embankments and elegant bridges is one of the capital's major attractions.

KOTELNICHESKAYA EMBANKMENT on the left-hand bank of the Moskva River begins at the spot where the Yauza River flows into it. The embankment got its name after a small settlement, numbering seven houses, where crafts-

In the 1940s, the Kotelnicheskaya Embankment, just as the other embankments of the Moskva River, was clad in granite and its roadway was broadened and paved with asphalt.

In 1948-1952, a tall building—another "wedding-cake" skyscraper in the style known as Stalinist classicism—was built on Kotelnicheskaya Embankment at the spot where the Yauza, Moscow's second biggest river, flows into the Moskva River. The building was designed by architects D. N. Chechulin and A. K. Rostovsky and engineer L. M. Gokhman.

As is characteristic of the other post-war Moscow skyscrapers, its central 24-storey volume is arranged in tiers. The first five storeys form an imposing socle faced with granite. The top part of the building is decorated with obelisks, sculptural groups and figured parapets, which, when seen from a distance, seem to form a kind of a crown. The central volume of the complex, expressive in silhouette, is flanked by three towers that are smaller in height; they are supplemented with side wings overlooking the Moskva and Yauza Rivers.

Undoubtedly picturesque in silhouette, the building is well inscribed in the landscape of the river bend, visually replacing the Shvivaya Hill—one of Moscow's historical seven hills—situated behind it. Besides 700 flats, the building also houses a cinema and a number of shops.

**170.** *The "wedding-cake"*
*skyscraper*
*on Kotelnicheskaya*
*Embankment*

170

In the southwest of Moscow, on the Vorobyovy Hills, one of the highest points in the city—an elevation rising some 75 metres above the level of the Moskva River—stands the tall building of Lomonosov MOSCOW STATE UNIVERSITY, the biggest among the Moscow skyscrapers built in the 1950s. It was built to the design of the finest Moscow architects L. V. Rudnev, S. Ye. Chernyshev, P. V. Abrosimov, and A. F. Khryakov and engineer V. N. Nasonov.

The main tower of the university contains the departments of mathematics and geography, lecturers' and professors' flats, student dormitories, a scientific library, an auditorium seating 1,500, a student club, the University Museum, the university president's office, and the administrative arm of the university.

Both in its external décor and in its interior decoration natural stone–marble, limestone, granite, etc.–is widely used. The sculptures and reliefs decorating it abound in emblems of the Soviet period.

The complex of university buildings is very impressive. The university campus lying round its main tower, which together with the spire rises to a height of nearly 240 metres, includes 27

171
172

171 - 172. *Lomonosov Moscow State University*

173. *Monument to M.V. Lomonosov. The main building of Lomonosov Moscow State University on the Vorobyovy Hills*

main buildings, a number of sports facilities, botanical gardens, and a park. Together they form a superb architectural ensemble.

Of much interest is the gallery of sculptural portraits of prominent figures in Russian science and art, which is to be seen on the university grounds. The portraits include those of A. M. Butlerov, A. I. Herzen, N.Ye. Zhukovsky, N. I. Lobachevsky, D. I. Mendeleyev, I. V. Michurin, I.. P. Pavlov, K. A. Timiryazev, N. G. Cherbyshevsky, and others.

In the centre of the main courtyard in front of the main tower stands a bronze statue of the great Russian scientist Mikhail Lomonosov after whom the university is named (sculptor N. V. Tomsky).

174

**174.** *The Ploshchad Revolyutsii Metro station*

**175.** *The entrance hall of the Krasniye Vorota Metro station*

**176.** *The ground-level entrance hall of the Kropotkinskaya Metro station*

**177.** *The pavilion of the Arbatskaya Metro station*

175

**178.** *The Battle of Borodino Panorama Museum. Monument to M. I. Kutuzov*

offers us a chance to see the changes we have lived through in this 20th century of ours: we are only to travel from station to station, changing from one line to another.

The first train of the Moscow Metro ran on May 15, 1935, when the first thirteen stations of its first line were opened. Over a period of more than half a century, the total length of its lines has increased nearly twentyfold. Today it has some 200 stations. Every day seven million people—and on some days, nine million people or more—use the services of the Moscow Metro.

The entrance to the Krasniye Vorota (Red Gate) Station is made to look like a shell. The pylons of the station are faced with red, white, yellow and grey marble. The station walls are faced with red and grey marble and the floor is covered with red and grey floor tiles.

Situated in the very centre of Moscow is the Ploshchad Revolyutsii (Revolution Square) Metro Station, which was opened to passenger traffic in March 1938. The colour palette of its marble facing includes black, red, light-golden, white, and grey. Near the pylons—massive pillars supporting the ceilings and vaults—and next to the passageways stand 76 bronze statues.

THE MOSCOW METRO is a veritable underground city. Ranging from very spacious, high, light, lavishly decorated stations arousing our admiration to simple, unpretentious ones designed for use rather than beauty, built in the past few years, some of them faced with rare varieties of stone and others, with steel and glass, the Metro

The Kropotkinskaya Metro Station, one of the oldest in Moscow, was put into service in May 1935. Its entrance is a smoothly curved arch supported by massive columns faced with valuable varieties of stone. The columns and walls inside the station are faced with light marble and the floor is covered with pink and grey granite.

The Arbatskaya Metro Station was opened to passenger traffic at the same time as the Kropotkinskaya Station. Its ground vestibule is made in the shape of a five-pointed star. It has festive-looking interiors with a high ceiling supported by two rows of columns and walls faced with white and grey ceramic tiles.

In 1962, to mark the 150th anniversary of the Battle of Borodino (1812), a building was erected to the design of architects A. P. Korabelnikov, A. A. Kuzmin and S. I. Kuchanov and engineer Yu. Ye. Avrutin specially for displaying the Battle of BORODINO PANORAMA created by the artist Franz Roubaud in 1912.

In 1973, a monument to Mikhail Kutuzov by sculptor N. V. Tomsky and architect L. G. Golubovsky was put up in front of the museum. The equestrian statue of the field marshal stands on a high granite pedestal surrounded with bronze images of Russian war heroes in high relief.

176

177

178

The monument to Yuri Gagarin in Gagarin Square was unveiled in 1980. Its 40 metre high silvery pedestal is reminiscent of the fiery tail of a rocket leaving the earth, with the globe at its foot. At the top of the monument is a full-length figure of Yuri Gagarin wearing a space-suit, with his arms spread like wings.

**179.** *Monument to Yuri Gagarin*

## THE ALL-RUSSIA EXHIBITION CENTRE (former USSR Economic Achievements Exhibition) was set up in 1959 on the basis of three previously existing exhibitions—an industrial, an agricultural and a construction exhibition. It was first opened in 1939 as an All-Union Agricultural Exhibition.

The Exhibition Centre is, above all, a unique monument of Soviet architecture abounding in symbols of the period of the 1930s through 1950s—structures, fountains and minor forms that transfer the visitor, as it were, into the

180

**180.** *The Friendship of the Peoples Fountain at the All-Russia Exhibition Centre*

Stalinist period. It is a vast park covering an area of more than 200 hectares. It is also a whole township consisting of 80 pavilions and 200 other facilities for recreation and amusement.

One of the main squares of the Exhibition Centre wonder township is Friendship of the Peoples Square. Its adornment—and the adornment of the whole Exhibition—is a great fountain of the same name. The extravaganza of water jets spurting from an enormous golden sheaf of wheat is surrounded by fifteen bronze figures of girls.

In all, fourteen fountains line the alley leading from the arch of the Main Entrance, topped with a sculptural group, to the Central Pavilion.

179

**181.** *The arch of the Main Entrance to the All-Russia Exhibition Centre. Detail*

126

THE NESKUCHNY (LEISURE) GARDEN with its undulating groves and glades on picturesque hillsides is the oldest part of the Gorky Central Amusement Park stretching on the bank of the Moskva River over an area of 100 hectares (set up in 1928 on the site of the former All-Russia Agricultural Exhibition and the Handicraft and Industry Exhibition of 1923, the Neskuchny Garden and the Vorobyovy Hills). Grown with maples, limes, poplars and willows, the park is noted for its ponds, flowerbeds, fountains and picturesque alleys decorated with sculptures. Its eastern part has been made into an amusement area. Beyond the Neskuchny Garden, near Pushkinskaya Embankment, stands the immense amphitheatre of the Zelyony (Green) Theatre, one of the biggest open-air theatres in Moscow.

Superbly designed embankments of the Moskva River (architect A. V. Vlasov) with beautiful descents leading to the water and a rotunda summerhouse are an integral part of the park.

**182.** *The rotunda summerhouse in the Neskuchny (Leisure) Garden*

**183.** *The "Luzhkov Bridge," a new pedestrian bridge in the Zamoskvorechye*

**184.** *The Crimean Bridge*

There are many beautiful railings and grilles adorning Moscow's boulevards, gardens, houses, parks and bridges. A fence of rare beauty—an excellent example of mid-18th century Russian foundry work—is the main attraction of the former A. P. Demidov's mansion at 3 Bolshoi Tolmachevsky Lane. It is believed to be produced at the Demidovs' works in Nizhni Tagil by master founder T. S. Sizov in the 1760s. The grille of the fence is lavishly ornamented with a rich floral pattern. Very expressive and quite inimitable is the cast-iron décor of the fence.

The superb metal fence in the inner courtyard of the Russia Insurance Society's tenant house in Sretensky Boulevard is a fine example of late 19th-century Russian wrought-iron grilles.

Amidst a housing project on the bank of the Moskva River, one unexpectedly comes into view of an island of green. It is the Krasnaya Presnya Park opened in 1932. In the 18th century, the Studenets Estate of the Princes Gagarin was situated here.

**185.** *The wrought-iron fence of A. P. Demidov's manor in Bolshoi Tolmachevsky Lane*

**186.** *The metal fence of the Russia Insurance Society's tenant house in Sretensky Boulevard*

**187.** *A bridge in the Krasnaya Presnya Park*

**188.** *A pedestrian bridge over the Yauza River*

Today a number of pavilions for conducting international exhibitions have been built on the park grounds.

Flowing through Moscow is the Yauza River, a left-hand tributary of the Moskva River. At one time it was a full-flowing river with numerous dams and water mills. Gradually, however, it became more and more shallow and muddy. In the 1930s, its bed was straightened and made nearly twice as wide as it used to be. Today small vessels can navigate the Yauza River within the city limits. The banks of the river have been covered with granite and a number of railroad and motor-road bridges and two Metro bridges have been built across it. And yet two footbridges across the Yauza are the most attractive.

КИЕВСКИЙ ВОКЗАЛ

189

190

A long time ago, people entered and left Moscow through the gates of what was known as the Earthworks City, the White City and Kitaigorod. Today other routes lead to Moscow—by rail, road, air, and water. The capital has nine railroad stations, four airports, and two river ports.

The Yaroslavl Station began its history as a small building erected in 1862. In the early 20th century, the modest building was replaced by a beautiful station combining motifs of Art Nouveau and traditions of North Russian architecture.

In 1965, the station underwent reconstruction and enlargement. A new building with glass walls was built on to its back near the platforms. The Yaroslavl Station is the starting point of the Trans-Siberian Railway stretching for 9,300 kilometres to the Pacific Coast. Trains going to Arkhangelsk, Murmansk and Vorkuta in the north of Russia also leave from this station.

The Kiev Station, built between 1913 and 1917, is an example of innovation in architecture and of a search for daring, creative design solu-

**189.** *The Kiev Railway Station*

**190.** *The Kazan Railway Station*

tions. Its building is a typical example of neo-classicism. The central part of the station reminds one of a gallery with Romanesque windows and Ionic columns. The building is flanked on either side by a massive wing framed with twin columns, adorned with sculptures and topped with a dome. A massive tower with a clock completes the composition of the building, making it look like a palace. Great metal arches above part of the platforms support an immense glass vault.

The Northern River Port is one of Moscow's attractions. It was built in the style known as Stalinist classicism in 1937, after the opening of the Moskva-Volga Canal (it took four years and eight months to build this 128 kilometres long canal). This graceful round-ended building with terraces arranged in tiers resembles a three-deck ship that seems to be sailing on land.

The décor of its façade incorporates an unusual element—round relief polychrome ceramic panels with representations of various means of transport and contemporary buildings.

A wide grand staircase leads down from the building to the quay, and the entire port grounds are a beautiful park.

191

**191.** *The Northern River Port in Khimki*

**192.** *The Yaroslavl Railway Station*

192

KRASNOPRESNENSKAYA EMBANKMENT is one of the central embankments of the Moskva River. Besides comfortable multi-storey blocks of flats, there are a number of public buildings here.

Situated on this embankment is the International Trade Centre with its offices and exhibition pavilions. At the spot where the embankment borders on New Arbat Street, stands the 105 metres high tower of Moscow City Hall. This light, festive-looking building opens the panorama of New Arbat Street. This 32-storey tower has a distinctive shape—two curved wings linked by a lift shaft, making it look like an enormous open book.

Besides the office building, the Moscow City Hall complex includes a 13-storey hotel. The complex was designed by architects M. Posokhin, A. Mndoyants and V. Svirsky. The office building was designed by architects S. Yegorov and Yu. Semyonov and the hotel building, by M. Pershin.

The focal point of the entire complex of buildings on the embankment is the Russian Federation Government House (the White House).

**193.** *Krasnopresnenskaya Embankment*

Designed by architects D. N. Chechulin, P. P. Shteller and others, it was completed by 1980.

The 20-storey building of the White House faced with white marble is strictly symmetrical in shape and built in a pyramidal fashion. A broad grand staircase leads from the embankment to the main entrance. In silhouette, the centre of the composition is emphasised with a clock tower mounted on which is a gilt representation of the state emblem of Russia. On top of the tower is a flagstaff with the Russian state flag.

Vertically the building is divided into two main parts—a lower, seven-storey part with side wings and an auditorium on the northern side and a central, 20-storey part topped with a service storey that has narrow vertical windows. The ceremonial section of the complex faces the Moskva River.

The building, fitted out with state-of-the-art equipment, has numerous offices, conference halls and meeting rooms perfectly suited for the work of an official government body.

Moscow is rapidly changing its appearance: old buildings and architectural monuments are being restored and, at the same time, new buildings conforming to the most up-to-date standards, are being built.

THE PRESIDENT HOTEL, built in the 1980s, is situated in Bolshaya Yakimanka Street in the central part of the city.

New banks and their branches have established themselves in and round the centre of the city amidst residential districts and lent an absolutely new appearance to traditional Moscow streets. One of the new buildings of the complex of Russian and international banks in Masha Poryvayeva Street is the building of the International Investment Bank.

The old Balchug Hotel in the Zamoskvorechye was one of the first to be modernised and turned into a classical European hotel which is a member of the World Leading Hotels Association.

**194.** *The President Hotel (also known as the Oktyabrskaya Hotel)*

**195.** *The International Investment Bank in Masha Poryvayeva Street*

**196.** *The old Balchug Hotel*

194

195

**197.** *The stadium*

*in Luzhniki*

**198.** *Arbat Street*

OLD ARBAT STREET is a street sung in many songs. It is bustling with activity at any time of day, and it is in Arbat Street that artists, musicians, lovers of poetry and amateur songwriters like to get together.

Arbat Street is first mentioned in the chronicles of the year 1493. Its name is a word of Oriental origin and means a district lying outside the city walls, a suburb. At the time Arbat began right at the Troitskaya Tower of the Kremlin. After the walls of the White City were erected this part of Moscow was no longer a suburb and the name was given to the street lying outside the Arbat Gates.

In the second half of the 18th century, when members of the nobility began to take up residence in Ostozhenka, Prechistenka and Povarskaya Streets and the neighbourhood began to turn into what Alexander Herzen wittily dubbed "Moscow's Saint-Germain suburb," Arbat also became a fashionable aristocratic street. At the same time, unlike the neighbouring streets, it was loud with life, for it was the only shopping street in this aristocratic isle: shops were not permitted to be opened in the other streets.

In Arbat Street and the neighbouring side streets quite a few buildings associated with the names of A. I. Herzen, K. F. Ryleyev, A. S. Pushkin, M. Yu. Lermontov, N. V. Gogol, and other prominent figures in Russian culture have survived. As is known, in Moscow on February 18, 1831, Pushkin married beautiful Natalia Goncharova, whom he deeply and passionately loved. After the wedding they lived for some months in a flat on the first floor at No. 53, in a house which now has quite a modern look. It was a very happy period in Pushkin's life… This was the poet's only flat in Moscow. Today it is the Alexander Pushkin Memorial Museum and the flat has been made to look like it did in the poet's lifetime more than a century and a half ago.

There are many side streets off Arbat, which were undoubtedly familiar to Pushkin in his day. In particular, he visited the Church of Our Saviour-on-the-Sands in Spasopeskovsky Lane. This 17th-century modest Arbat church with an open-work belfry is depicted in the painting A Moscow Side Street by the noted artist Polenov.

The Renaissance (Olympic-Penta) Hotel is one of the best hotels in Moscow. It has 472 first-class well-appointed guestrooms, 11 deluxe suites, and a presidential suite on the top floor. All the guestrooms and suites are equipped with international telephone lines, satellite television, individual heating and air conditioning, minibars, etc.

A 300-seat conference hall fitted out with equipment for simultaneous translation into five languages and various audio and video equipment, as well as 12 meeting rooms and banquet halls of different size are ideal for conducting business meetings, lunches and celebrations.

The hotel's facilities include restaurants, a health club with a swimming pool, a gym, a sauna, etc.

**199.** *The Renaissance (Olympic-Penta) Hotel*

199

of a wide central alley named "War Years," which ends before its façade in round Victors Square in the centre of which rises a 140 metres high obelisk (architects V. Budayev and L. Vavakin) crowned with a flying figure of Nike, the winged goddess of victory (sculptor Z. Tsereteli). The museum faces Victors Square with a semicircular pylonnade behind which is the building, square in plan, housing the main halls of the museum. To the left of the central alley stands the Church of St. George the Victorious, the patron saint of Moscow (1993-1995).

THE MOSCOW ZOO, the oldest one in Russia, was opened in 1864. It was founded by Count Bobrinsky and the noted Russian biologists K. F. Roulier, S. A. Usov, and others. Initially it had some 300 animals and now it has about 3,000.

Between 1990 and 1996, the Moscow Zoo underwent overall reconstruction (architect A. A. Andreyev), during which new enclosures and structures imitating natural features (an eagles' cliff, an antelopes' island, etc.) were built for its inhabitants. Particularly interesting is the new entrance with two fanciful turrets on the side of Krasnaya Presnya Street.

**200.** *The Memorial of the Victory in the Great Patriotic War of 1941–1945 on the Poklonnaya Hill*

**201.** *The central entrance to the Moscow Zoo*

THE MEMORIAL OF THE VICTORY IN THE GREAT PATRIOTIC WAR OF 1941-1945 stretches over an area of 20 hectares on the highest elevation of the Poklonnaya Hill in the Victory Park. This architectural ensemble, built in 1983-1995, includes a museum, several sculptural monuments, an open-air display, and a church. The building of the museum (architect A. T. Polyansky) is topped with a massive dome. One can get here from Kutuzovsky Prospekt by way

**202.** *The Central Telegraph Office, a glass office building and a MacDonald's restaurant in Tverskaya Street*

Present-day Moscow is yet to find its chroniclers. It is "inscribed" in isles of new buildings and districts into traditional Moscow, which was known as the "first-cathedra city" and "golden-domed Moscow." Over the past few years numerous monuments of Russian architecture—cathedrals, churches and old mansions—have been restored and an even greater number of them are now being restored. They include the Cathedral of Christ the Saviour, a magnificent 19th-century edifice which is a monument to the victory in the Patriotic War of 1812 and a symbol of the undying Orthodox faith. It took only a year to complete its main dome and today all of its five domes are already sparkling with gilt.

Robert Rozhdestvensky, the poet, noted once not without reason that a city is a dialogue between the past and the present. Moscow is today conducting such a dialogue with redoubled energy: while preserving love and respect for its past, it is striving to enter the next century as a renovated, modern city full of life and vigor. It combines in itself both the past and the present, and out of this combination shoots of the future are sprouting.

As is the long tradition in Russia, in preparation for celebrating its 850th anniversary Moscow has smoothed the wrinkles left on its face by its eventful past, preened itself, renovated its beauty and added some fresh colours to it.

The photographs in this album are only sketches for a portrait of Moscow. For not a single publication, however large it might be, can depict all the features of this great city. Founded as a small settlement on the Borovitsky Hill eight and a half centuries ago, Moscow has been progressing through the centuries, constantly renovating its appearance and augmenting its treasures, like a beautiful faerie who has uncovered the secret of eternal youth. And the "secret" of Moscow is simple: it is the true and undying love of many generations of Russians for their capital.

**203.** *Two towers near the Krasnokholmskaya Spit. The construction of the Russian Cultural Centre*

*Moscow*

Art-Rodnik, Moscow, 2001